Life's NEXT Path

Carol McGowan PhD

Published in 2025 by Strategic Achievement Coaching
Sydney, Australia
Contact: www.strategicachievementcoaching.com.au
Copyright © 2025 Dr Carol McGowan

Title: *Your NEXT Path*
Author: Dr Carol McGowan
PRINT ISBN: 9781764006804
EPUB ISBN: 9781764006811
Subjects: Personal Growth | Aging | Motivation & Inspiration

Book Production Services: www.smartwomenpublish.com
Registered with the National Library Australia

All rights reserved. No part of this book may be reproduced or transmitted in any form or by any means, electronic or mechanical, including photocopying, recording, scanning or information storage and retrieval system without the prior written consent of the publisher. No part of this book may be used by other parties without the author's prior written consent, for reproducing, publishing, communicating, or otherwise using the Work or any part of the Work to develop, train or direct Generative Artificial Intelligence technology or models ('Generative AI'), including but not limited to the mining or scraping of text, images or data from the Work.

Disclaimer:
The material in this publication is of the nature of general comment only and does not represent professional advice. All material is provided for educational purposes only. We recommend to always seek the advice of a qualified professional before making any decision regarding personal and business needs. To the maximum extent permitted by law, the author and publisher disclaim all responsibility and liability to any person arising directly or indirectly from any person taking or not taking action based on the information in this publication.

YOUR PATH THROUGH THIS BOOK

Meet the Author. 9
Introduction
    The Intention of This Book 13
    Take Action with This Book 19
Chapter 1: Your Story is Calling You 29
    Know how to define and describe yourself 32
    Your ability to change 40
    Your willingness to change 44
    Your capacity to change – enablers and barriers 47
Chapter 2: Making a Change – Why now? 53
    What has occurred? 55
    What are you experiencing? 59
    What is the consequence of doing something? 63
    What is the consequence of doing nothing? 66
Chapter 3: Start Here 71
    What is doable? 74
    Find a starting point. 79
    Determine the merit of your starting point 83
    What else do you need to think about?. 86

Chapter 4: Slaying the Saboteurs 91
Values and beliefs (enabling and limiting) *94*
Strengths and how to leverage them *101*
Saboteurs *106*
Understanding meaning and purpose. *111*
Describing yourself and self-related attitudes. *117*

Chapter 5: Pack Your Bag. 125
Learn to speak up for yourself *127*
SIMPLE goal setting. *132*
The secret to changing habits. *142*
From to-do to Ta-Da *146*
Spiritual self-care and why it matters *151*
Review your travel bag. *155*

Chapter 6: Success – What Does It Look Like? 161
Success criteria. *162*
Measuring success. *170*
Developing reflective practices. *172*
Keeping your intentions in sight *178*
Staying on track. *182*

Chapter 7: Celebrate Success. 191
Why celebrate success? *193*
The benefits of celebrating with others *197*
Celebration frequency and type *202*

Bringing It All Together 209
Strategic intent *209*
Strategic action *211*
Strategic intuition *213*

Conclusion: Set Forth. 217

Invitation from Carol 219

Acknowledgements 221

LIST OF EXERCISES

Chapter 1
    Exercise 1: Starting to Tell Your Story *38*
    Exercise 2: Determining Your Ability to Change *43*
    Exercise 3: Assessing Your Willingness to Change *46*
    Exercise 4: Evaluating Your Capacity to Change *49*

Chapter 2
    Exercise 5: Discerning Why Now Is the
    Right Time to Act *58*
    Exercise 6: Reviewing Feelings *61*
    Exercise 7: Features of Desired Change *65*
    Exercise 8: Consequences of Choosing Not to Act *67*

Chapter 3
    Exercise 9: Steps for Making Change *77*
    Exercise 10 : Determining a Meaningful
    Starting Point. *81*
    Exercise 11: Reviewing Enablers and Barriers *85*
    Exercise 12: Critical Review of Starting Point *88*

Chapter 4
    Exercise 13a: Identifying Your Values *98*
    Exercise 13b: Identifying Your Beliefs *99*
    Exercise 14: Identifying Your Signature Strengths *104*
    Exercise 15: Revealing Your Saboteurs *109*

Exercise 16: Discerning Meaning 115
Exercise 17: Understanding Your
Self-Related Attitudes 120

Chapter 5
Exercise 18: Task Assessment. 130
Exercise 19: SIMPLE SMART Goal Development 138
Exercise 20: Become Intentional 145
Exercise 21: Developing a Ta-Da List 150
Exercise 22: How You Nurture Your
Spiritual Wellbeing 154
Exercise 23: Resource Inventory 157

Chapter 6
Exercise 24: Confirming Your SIMPLE SMART
Goals 164
Exercise 25: Determining Success Criteria 171
Exercise 26: Reflective Practices Worksheet 175
Exercise 27: Setting Intentions:
Sentence-Completion Activity 180
Exercise 28: Setting up a Personal
Accountability Framework 185

Chapter 7
Exercise 29: Achievements Log 195
Exercise 30: Achievement Celebration Guide –
Part 1. 200
Exercise 31: Achievement Celebration Guide –
Part 2 205

Bringing it all Together
Exercise 32: Amalgamate Chapters 1–4
(Your Intent) 210
Exercise 33: Amalgamate Chapters 5–7
(Your Action) 212
Exercise 34: Your Intuition 213

This book is dedicated to Frank McGowan, who provided unconditional earthly love and support, and God, who provided divine guidance, strength, and courage.

To both, thank you. I could not have achieved this without you.

MEET THE AUTHOR

In my earlier career, I trained as an accountant but later reinvented myself as a coach and counsellor to satisfy and honour my desire to lead a meaningful life and make a difference through my work. To achieve that change, I gained a diploma in positive psychology, a master's degree in coaching, and a PhD exploring what makes great people excel in their chosen field.

But my greatest qualification for writing this book about finding your next path is that I've had to live and learn exactly the ideas and skills that I share in these pages. I have undergone two significant transformations in my life – the first by choosing to make a dramatic career change at fifty, and the second by responding to difficult circumstances when my husband passed away in March 2020.

By fifty, I had become stuck in my career and was no longer finding fulfilment in the work I was doing, which was data-oriented, so I decided to change course and become a coach, counsellor, and adult educator.

I needed to start from a zero base of knowledge and experience in that specific field and rebuild my professional reputation in a whole new area of expertise, knowledge, and skills. This was scary. But if I had stayed where I was, the extreme downsides of being stuck would have come into play. I would have become frustrated and despondent, leading to a life where I was simply existing and not experiencing the radiant and radical fulfilment I sought.

Later, when I became a widow, I had to face a transformation without my personal guiding light, my husband. I had no choice but to become my own torch for the latter stage of my life. This transformation has led me to capture what I've learned and pour it into this book. The concepts and approaches I share here emerged along the way as I learned to live life flying solo.

I trust what I have learned is useful as you find your own next path too.

Dr Carol McGowan
Strategic Achievement Coaching
Sydney, Australia

Introduction

THE INTENTION OF THIS BOOK

To someone outside looking in, you may have already succeeded in life. Maybe you have the job you always wanted; you have material possessions that mean something to you; or you have the family you always dreamed of.

However, something is nagging at you.

You know you're at a point where you're seeking to make a meaningful life change or transition, either personally or professionally. You desire to find purpose and fulfilment beyond your current achievements.

This can bring about a mix of difficult emotions, including frustration, fear, indecision, uncertainty, loss of focus, grief, or inexplicable sadness.

It is also possible that you feel excitement, a sense of expectation, and enthusiasm for what comes next. Whatever your feelings, they are all valid and likely indicators that you are ready to head off on your next path.

What you do know with certainty is that you need more direction and focus to figure out what to do next.

To paraphrase popular author and career counsellor, Barbara Sher: You know you can do anything if only you knew what that is. I have been there myself and have now written this book to help you find what it takes to make the shift you want. This is the book I wish I had had at that time.

When you start something new, the uncertainty associated with change is scary. You might be justifiably concerned about the risks involved in shifting your career or life path at this stage in your life. You're wondering how to take those risks in a way that is sensible and diminishes or eliminates the potential uncertainty involved.

If you've reached the point where you want to make a change and you're not sure what to do, chances are you feel stuck – and that is not a comfortable place to stay in for too long. It can be debilitating and feel awful if not given proper attention. Maybe what used to feel good no longer feels that way anymore. You're even wondering if you want to take the risk of change to pursue purpose and meaning.

The reality is, if you choose to pursue something different and new, you'll have more at stake if by chance you don't succeed. You can ignore the push and pull to shift from being stuck – it's easy. You just keep yourself busy, so you do not have to think about it – but at what cost?

INTRODUCTION: THE INTENTION OF THIS BOOK

Unfortunately, there is a price to pay if you do nothing, and that can include:

- Despair
- Resignation that nothing can or will change
- The sad thought that this is as good as it gets
- A sense of hopelessness and the defeat of thinking *why bother*

None of these thoughts, if allowed to persist for a long period, will be good for your health and wellbeing.

Instead, I want the insights in this book to help ensure you know how to successfully pull off the change you want, without regrets.

It is reassuring to know you are not alone in this quest for more in your life. According to the article, 'Redesigning Retirement' by Ken Dychtwald, Robert Morison, and Katy Terveer (*Harvard Business Review*, March–April 2024):

> 'If "retirement" means completely ceasing work and devoting two or more decades to 24/7 leisure, it's increasingly impractical, unappealing, and obsolete. Two-thirds of older Americans now view retirement not as a time of pure rest and relaxation but as a new chapter in life, with plenty of room for new ambitions and renewed purpose.'

* * *

First, let me tell you how I got started with this idea of life's next path, and what I learned along the way.

On 11 March 2020, the same day COVID-19 was declared a global pandemic, I became a widow. I lost the love of my life, my rock, and the most influential person who contributed to my personal growth and development. How could I ever move on from this?

Although I'm a capable person, this was the first time in my life I had to live alone permanently. My grief was intense. My lifeline was gone. Processing what was happening – and knowing that my husband was a life-goes-on person and wishing to honour him – I took steps to work actively and deliberately towards developing Carol 3.0.

Carol 1.0 was my childhood. Carol 2.0 was the time I was with my husband (forty-one years). Carol 3.0 was the five-year transition period spent coming to terms with my loss, learning to live life solo, and determining who I am now.

I am now Carol 4.0, in the process of becoming the best Carol I can be, continuing to grow and evolve as I traverse this next path in my life. This stage is informed by what has gone before, but is extremely different in its focus, as I have the freedom to choose what those previous iterations of Carol had not provided, acknowledging that each version was rich and fulfilling in their own unique way.

INTRODUCTION: THE INTENTION OF THIS BOOK

Remember, this is about finding the right next path for you now.

I did not use the term 'next path' when I started my process of recovery from the loss of my husband. The task seemed impossible, but somewhere I found a small granule of determination to hold on to by taking time to hear my voice buried beneath all the grief. I had counselling; I harnessed the strength of my support crew and the promises of my faith; and I went on a voyage to find the next version of Carol. Along the way, I discovered things that worked for me and others, both clients and friends. As I think about it now, I see that the path to Carol 4.0 snuck up on me when I was not looking.

I also ardently believe it is never too late to have a purpose in your life. My difficult experience was the major contributor to finding my life's next path when I thought personal regeneration would be impossible. Let me tell you, it is not. With the right mindset and support, you can do it.

Engaging in activities that challenge your mind—such as learning new skills, staying active, engaging in creativity, and enjoying positive experiences—helps form other new pathways too.

The new neural pathways you are forming enhance neuroplasticity, the brain's ability to reorganise by creating new connections. This process supports cognitive flexibility, memory, and problem-solving, all essential for maintaining mental sharpness as we age. Strengthening these connections promotes brain health, delays cognitive decline, and keeps you feeling mentally agile and resilient – helping you stay young at heart and mind.

* * *

I passionately believe – no, I know – that you can find a new and exciting path in your life and achieve what you want. This book will help you do that more easily by providing insights and exercises to help you, and by giving you a way to change your life with the highest possible chance of success – and the least possible likelihood of risk, major detours, or disasters.

This book will provide you with a list of practical steps and activities (as you make your way through the exercises in this book), and the way to your NEXT path will become clearer and clearer. There will also be challenging steps that require deep thinking. The insights in this book will show you how to do that, and how to successfully make your way to the next big thing in your life.

Most importantly, enjoy making time for you to do what you find fulfilling.

TAKE ACTION WITH THIS BOOK

You've achieved success in your life so far, and you are reading this book because you're eager to do more and achieve your next big thing. While breaking a big goal into smaller steps makes it more manageable, the details can sometimes obscure the bigger picture. A clear framework can help you stay focused on your ultimate goal as you take each step toward your next success.

Over the last twenty years, I have experienced an extensive and intensive learning process. The biggest lessons have come from life, rather than any formal studies. These lessons, sourced from my own experience and that of my clients, have led me to develop the Strategic Achievement Framework to help people formulate and implement purposeful, helpful, and, more importantly, fulfilling life strategies.

Using this framework has enabled those I have worked with to determine their next path, then navigate their way in a meaningful and purposeful way, leading to a sense of fulfilment they had not thought possible. If you'd like to join this group of people living a fulfilled life, this book will help you do that.

The steps in this book are offered in a sequence that will assist you to move from stuck to free, allowing you to achieve your next desired result. It is informed by the framework I developed, which consists of three key components: intent, action, and intuition. The following diagram provides a visual representation:

The framework offers an integrated approach to finding a new direction most effectively. It enhances the likelihood of experiencing renewed fulfilment and having experiences you never imagined possible. It ensures you adopt an integrated approach to getting what you want in life, rather than having a fragmented and disconnected one.

INTRODUCTION: TAKE ACTION WITH THIS BOOK

While each part of the framework has value on its own, they are even more powerful when combined. Each step you take will help inform the next – each iteration is like an upward spiral taking you closer to your desired destination.

Let's look at the individual words in the framework and then pull them together:

- Strategic: Considering long-term goals and objectives and how to reach them
- Achievement: Something accomplished using effort, expertise, and often courage
- Framework: A basic structure or system underlying a concept or approach that can lead to a desired outcome

The Strategic Achievement Framework (SAF) supports focused effort with expertise and courage as required, for the long-term achievement of goals. It is a practice-based-evidence approach that enables you to keep your eye on the long-term goal and not get overwhelmed by the details. It brings together the three powerful forces of intent, action, and intuition to deliver the shift you want to make.

Applying the Strategic Achievement Framework ensures that actions and goals are purposefully aligned with your genuine desires and are more likely to be achieved through intrinsically inspired choices and decisions.

COMPONENTS OF THE FRAMEWORK

Strategic Intent

Strategic intent is the process of identifying a desired direction or path, clearly defining the destination, and setting out a map of where you would like to go. We explore what makes that destination important. Strategic intent is your orientation toward goals. Setting your intention at the start of your journey lays the foundation for creating action plans later. This stage is all about seeing the big picture and being creative.

Strategic intent means becoming clear about the end result you desire, and being flexible as to the means of achieving it. Understanding, identifying, and harnessing the intent of your next path can lead to motivation, inspiration, focus, and sustainability.

Plans without strategic intent risk being misguided and insubstantial; intent married with intuition, though, can lead to purposeful action.

Strategic Action

What do you want your life to look like? As a coach, I help support individuals as they take stock of helpful and unhelpful behaviours, thoughts, and patterns.

In the process, they form a deeper understanding of what they want and intend for their life. They clarify

INTRODUCTION: TAKE ACTION WITH THIS BOOK

what they want to work towards, and then it's time to ask: What will you do to make it happen?

As I work with clients, we move from intent to action through positive goal setting. We tap into intuition to ensure these goals and resultant actions align with the clients' unique purpose and circumstances.

Strategic Intuition

In his book, *The Intuition Toolkit: The New Science of Knowing What without Knowing Why,* Joel Pearson, Australia's world-expert neuroscientist and professor at the University of New South Wales, and an eminent researcher on intuition, describes it as 'the learned productive use of unconscious information to improve decisions and actions'.

Strategic intuition helps you make sense of new situations, and make decisions that align with your intent and goals.

Intuition is often dismissed or disregarded simply because many do not understand it correctly. I like to think of this: if the entire system is a car, intent is the direction you intend to travel, action is petrol, with intuition being the oil. Intuition is just as crucial to progression as having a direction to go and petrol in the tank, but it does not often get the same degree of consideration as the other two factors. It helps to understand that the oil is drawn upon and refilled less often because it is more powerful and concentrated – but it is a critical ingredient for a successful outcome.

Intuition aids decision-making immensely because we do not usually have all the data points necessary to make truly informed decisions. Our intuition helps us as it never lets us down. As a coach, I help you access your intuition to give you essential input in your path to achievement.

Remember, however, that intuition and gut feelings are not the same thing. In his work, Joel Pearson states that gut feelings are survival instincts acting as an immediate response to an external trigger or stimuli, whereas intuition is a reliable guide for making informed choices, stemming from a higher level of consciousness. In short, strategic intuition provides wise responses and choices rather than reactive ones.

To tap into your intuition, you need to first understand your own story and be willing to stop long enough to hear your own voice. Understanding and applying intuition is the foundation of my Strategic Achievement Framework (SAF), and a feature that distinguishes it from most other coaching frameworks, which seem to predominantly focus on action.

Your intention and intuition are also critical components when determining what you do next. Each element is interactive and dynamic; however, your starting point is always your intention. The elements of the framework come together in a similar way to when you are making a trip while

INTRODUCTION: TAKE ACTION WITH THIS BOOK

considering weather conditions, distance to be travelled, and road conditions.

* * *

The development of the framework resulted from my experiences and reliance on my strategic intuition during a difficult time. On 21 September 2021, about eighteen months after I lost my husband, I thought about what I'd been doing to cope, and make goals for the next stage of my life. I thought about writing a book, and while considering what it might be about, the Strategic Achievement Framework came to life.

The first two components were easy – strategic intent and strategic action. Yet while I was pondering these two elements, I knew something was missing. I had not realised it was my strategic intuition at this point. Sitting with my discontent and allowing my intuition to kick in, the importance of using strategic intuition came to light. I shared my ideas about the framework with clients and professional colleagues over the next several months and they all said, 'This makes perfect sense.'

This framework was developed and informed as I used it with people developing their plans to reach their next important goal. As I gathered positive feedback on the merits of this framework, I began using it more deliberately with my clients, giving them time and encouraging them to use their intuition. We were all keen to see what would happen.

A crucial component was encouraging clients to listen with their eyes, not just their ears; our intuition is enhanced when we absorb information through all our senses. This method has led many clients to set goals that resonate with their intentions and align with their actions, without becoming bogged down by the details. Achieving the desired shift requires the interplay of three powerful forces: intent, action, and intuition, with intuition being the key element that makes the difference.

The table below shows how each of the chapters in this book relates to the components of the Strategic Achievement Framework.

Chapter Cross-Reference to Strategic Achievement Framework

INTUITION	INTENT	ACTION
Chapter 1		
	Chapter 2	
	Chapter 3	
Chapter 4		
	Chapter 5	
	Chapter 6	
		Chapter 7

INTRODUCTION: TAKE ACTION WITH THIS BOOK

When coaching clients who feel stuck, I often help them zoom out from the immediate steps and revisit the broader framework to understand where they are on their journey and how everything fits together. For example, Patricia (from Chapter 2) was deeply focused on her actions aligned with her current goals, but she started to feel overwhelmed. We paused and revisited the framework to remind her that she had already clearly defined her intent, which could guide the SIMPLE SMART goals she was developing. This shift in perspective allowed Patricia to fully leverage the work she had done so far.

Unexpectedly, this also sparked her intuition, leading to new insights that made her goals even more aligned with her true aspirations. She began to see connections and possibilities that hadn't been apparent before.

* * *

If you're aiming to achieve even greater success, this framework will be your guide, helping you reach that next goal and attain the profound fulfilment you're striving for.

Author note: You can download free life navigation resources and the first three exercises in this book (a fillable pdf) here: www.strategicachievementcoaching.com.au/resources

YOUR STORY IS CALLING YOU

The starting point for your journey along your next path is hearing and understanding your own story. It is the opportunity for you to notice what you are saying about yourself and how you've got to where you are. Hearing your own story enables you to identify what you are focusing on, what you're leaving out, and how you interpret what has taken place in your life.

This is not about the stories others tell about you; it is about the stories you tell about yourself. When you tell stories about yourself, you can experience a sense of release, and there is a power in feeling that your story is being heard, but most importantly, heard by you. This is not about telling a pretty story, it's about telling your 'real' story.

The simple act of articulating your story honestly, authentically, and purposefully will enable you to gain new perspectives and clarity. While those qualities are aligned and compatible, they are also different. Honesty is being both truthful and transparent; authenticity is being true to yourself; and purposefulness is about identifying a clear direction and intention to guide what you want to do. Each of these is crucial to finding the right place to start.

By tuning into and hearing your own story, you'll get better at identifying what you need to focus on, and what you might need to do to move towards your life's next path. This path can offer you the opportunity to feel more alive and whole than you ever have before.

No doubt there have been many paths followed, and paths left unexplored in your life so far, some taken instinctively or without guidance, some not. This book will act like a sherpa helping you to take meaningful steps on the next path you determine is right for you, taking you in the direction you choose to go.

Purposefully choosing a next path gives you a renewed sense of being alive and in control in later life. You now have the time and freedom to make decisions for yourself about the life you want, and you can take deliberate and purposeful actions to achieve that.

Through hearing your own stories now, you will have the opportunity to understand what matters to you at this time – those things that may not be so obvious. Our stories have links to what we desire, whether we're aware of them or not.

1: YOUR STORY IS CALLING YOU

Dr David Drake is a preeminent pioneer researcher of narrative coaching, and has facilitated transformative change for many people for over twenty years, using their stories in unique ways. In his book, *Narrative Coaching*, Drake makes the following comment:

> 'These self-defining memories [or stories] retain their emotional power because they are genuinely linked to goals and desires people consciously or unconsciously believe are still important for them.'

By listening to, and understanding your own voice through your life stories, your goals, desires, and aspirations are more likely to surface, and help inform how you may wish to travel along your next path. This helps you lay a solid foundation for what comes next.

Let's now explore and explain the value and relevance of hearing your own story, because how you portray yourself in your story provides insight into your current circumstances. You will see how understanding your story helps you determine a willingness to change, and an exploration of enablers and barriers helps you review your capacity to change.

In the following chapters, you will:

- Explore why now is the right time to act
- Identify what you want to start with
- Learn how to hear and benefit from your guiding voice

- Identify the right gear and equipment to include in your travel bag
- Understand the need to have strategically placed checkpoints to determine the route you wish to take
- Celebrate success along the way

KNOW HOW TO DEFINE AND DESCRIBE YOURSELF

Humans are superb storytellers, keeping cultural traditions alive over vast periods of time. We love listening to other people's stories, and yet we rarely, if ever, take time to listen to our own.

Knowing how to define and describe yourself means examining your story from your own perspective and not taking others' views into account. We all carry stories that have come to us from various people – our parents, siblings, friends, and other influential people we may encounter in life. Now, it's time to become conscious of those external stories and cast them off so you can focus on how you tell your own.

The risk of not telling your story is insufficient identity formation, the process where you develop your understanding of who you are and how you fit into your world. Telling your story is an act of generosity to yourself and others. By giving yourself and others the chance to explore your story allows for a better understanding of who you are. It helps

1: YOUR STORY IS CALLING YOU

you and others to connect to the essence of you. It is a mechanism that binds us together and assists you with making sense of your experience.

Often, a story will not feel significant – whether it's about your family, where you grew up, or a funny experience – but the story has meaning for you, so it is important. Considering your own story is analogous to looking in the rear-view mirror of a car while driving; you gain a rear perspective on what has enabled you to get to a certain point. That will then assist with understanding where your starting point may need to be, to get where you want to go next. You will better understand why this is important as you progress through this book.

Most people struggle with change because they don't know where to start the process. You would never set off on a vacation without knowing where you want to end up. Knowing your starting point and your destination determines the route you want to take, and the time you need to set aside to get there. Likewise, the stories you tell about yourself and your experiences all help to inform the starting point for the journey you are about to embark on.

For many years, I refused to call myself a leader. I always wanted to be the backstop and not the visible one upfront. I happily described myself as a follower. Then, I took a loving challenge set by a friend who heard me describe myself as 'not a leader', which helped me to reconsider my perspective and acknowledge there are situations where I am a guide. Once I was willing to tell this new story, I could understand the impact of the old one, and how it was causing and contributing to my discomfort and discontent.

I'm now willing to accept that I am a leader in my chosen field, and I treat that honour with respect and pride. (As a somewhat ironic postscript, I now teach leadership at the postgraduate level.)

In the realm of social media today, many of us are regularly giving snippets of who we are to others, but these are most often selective highlights like, 'I had a great win at work today.' However, we leave out the details of the struggle and the tenacity it took to achieve the great win. It is only in telling your story in more depth that you provide yourself with important information regarding what you are capable of and what needs to change: 'I had a great win at work today. I had to draw on my tenacity and perseverance to achieve the win, even when reaching the requirement by the stated deadline seemed impossible.'

If you only provide highlights of your story to fit in with others' expectations or to appear successful, you're going to lose the opportunity to give yourself information about what it takes to make change. The more detailed and truthful telling of your stories will include where you have made changes, both successfully and unsuccessfully. These are beneficial data points that contribute to your ability to make further changes you desire.

1: YOUR STORY IS CALLING YOU

You might think, 'My story isn't that interesting. I can't see how telling my story will be helpful.' We dismiss our past as boring or irrelevant, but it is our greatest asset. It's the history of our personal GPS that has formed as we have navigated life's trials. This is the best learning menu you will ever have, and you can add chapters you have crafted in the past and up to this point, as you travel your next path.

There may be parts of your story that are confronting to face and trigger responses, making it difficult to function. This can also apply to people who have experienced trauma or are suffering from a condition like PTSD – and any of the exercises outlined in this book could affect you that way.

I've learned this the hard way. There are certain personality types that trigger my fear of authority figures, and when I meet someone who affects me in this way, I want to shut down or escape and hide. In a meeting once, something triggered me, so during the break I stayed away for an hour until I could get myself back together. Later that afternoon, my manager took me to task for abandoning him in that way. He warned that if I ever did that again, he would need to take dramatic action as he considered my actions to be an example of poor performance.

To avoid this happening again, I had a meeting with my counsellor to discuss strategies I could use to help me stay physically present even if I felt the need to take an emotional time-out for a short while. A year later,

I was in a classroom studying for my master's degree when the lecturer belittled my point of view in front of the class. I felt humiliated and wanted to escape. However, using the strategies I had learned with my counsellor, I was able to physically stay present and give myself time to recalibrate emotionally. It took about fifteen minutes to do this, and then another opportunity arose to make my point and stay present.

My fellow students congratulated me after the class, saying they felt empowered to speak up because of observing my actions. I felt delighted that my courage, while aimed at my own wellbeing, had also inspired others to be brave.

If you have had experiences you found difficult, I recommend you speak with your mental-health professional, counsellor, therapist, or psychologist, and develop strategies that will enable you to do this in a way that ensures you stay psychologically safe, which is paramount.

Throughout this book, I will ask you to use a journal to complete exercises and also document your learnings. You will find those sections boxed in grey for easy recognition. There are two ways you can capture your journal responses:

1. In writing
2. By typing up your thoughts

My recommendation, based on my own experience and a variety of research studies, is to write things down; you will find it has many benefits. The following table will outline the benefit of writing things by hand rather than directly typing out your thoughts.

Benefits of Writing by Hand Rather than Typing

	Writing	Typing
1.	Makes learning easier by stimulating a unique neural pathway	A mechanical, repetitive process with restricted or limited learning benefits
2.	Can improve memory as it is *an assimilation process*	Limits retention as it is *a transaction process*
3.	Increases positive attachment to your journal with the likelihood of sustaining the practice for longer; portable and accessible; a more intimate process	Harder to do consistently if technical access is limited or unavailable
4.	Can be meditative as you can get lost in the writing, forgetting other concerns or considerations (removing distractions can help with this benefit)	Can seem like a work task given how widely technology is used in the workplace, making it difficult to distinguish it as a discrete activity
5.	Helps enhance creative expression e.g. drawing a mind map	Creative expression is constrained by the functionality of the software being used

Writing by hand will encourage a more extensive capturing of your own story than typing it up in the first instance. The portability means thoughts and ideas can be captured at any time, not just when you are near a computer or other electronic device. Writing things down also means you can potentially store them safely, whereas once a sentence is deleted from a device it's usually lost forever.

While I worked on the edits of this book, I completed them by hand before typing them up. This allowed a freer flow, and ensured I didn't lose or hinder key concepts because of any tech functionality.

EXERCISE 1

STARTING TO TELL YOUR STORY

Set aside fifteen minutes in a space where you're unlikely to be interrupted. It's beneficial to find a space you find calming – for example, your garden, by a river (a personal preference of mine), or in your favourite room in your house. Set the timer on your phone for fifteen minutes, then write things from your story that come to mind.

A few things might crop up quickly and then you might feel you've run out of steam. Stay the full fifteen minutes. Accept the gaps as natural, normal, and helpful. The gaps allow you to think of things that are deeper and more significant or relevant.

You might start with where you are today, where you've lived as a child, or a happy memory. There is no right or wrong about this. This is your opportunity to set aside time to hear your own story as the first step towards your next path. Try not to judge what you write. Just start somewhere. Every part of your story matters, like dots in an artwork. Alone, they don't seem like much, but when seen as a connected whole, the picture is not only beautiful but also compelling.

Remember, this is not a one-off activity. Do it as many times as you think you need.

You might also want to add a second phase to the activity, by melding the pieces together. If you decide to do this second phase, note:

- What are you noticing?
- What are the significant aspects of your story that are emerging?

Barriers that might arise are thoughts that your own story has no value, or feeling uncomfortable. Start small and only write for five minutes. Progress is progress, so just do something. Surprisingly, it will snowball. Don't overthink it; just let it flow.

You need to understand your past and present circumstances so you can fully understand your ability to change. This encompasses the physical, emotional, and psychological conditions of your life – they all impact your story, and how you see and describe yourself.

This is not about how much money you have, where you live, whether you are married, or where you work. You write about a particular point or circumstance that helps explain where you find yourself in life. There may be a point of discontent or discomfort where you feel stuck and want to make a shift. Or you may want to make a big change, but it seems overwhelming because of what is involved in making that change.

To illustrate, maybe you're always being overlooked for a promotion, even though you have an outstanding track record, a well-constructed resume, and you present well at interviews. The topic or issue you choose to write about to help you with this problem can be where you find yourself in the present moment, or a situation you have been in previously. Pick a point that has the most significance for you. Whatever you pick to focus on will become a part of helping you determine your ability to change.

Think about this. When someone writes a book, the published version is not the same as the first draft. Every book will undergo many edits before the final version is released to the world. But without the

1: YOUR STORY IS CALLING YOU

messy first draft, there's no possibility of a book. It is all just a pipe dream.

Equally important is understanding your own story and the circumstances in which you find yourself. These become a part of the first draft of your own story, a story of triumph rather than regret. When they are being written, books do not start on page one and finish with the conclusion. Usually, the author picks a starting point somewhere and then builds on it. The same applies to you picking a point to start your story. Creating order in any story comes later in the process.

When seeking to undertake change, there are three important considerations:

1. The ability to change – the skills, know-how, expertise, and resources that will help you facilitate change.
2. The willingness to change – a commitment to do something different, a desire to change.
3. The capacity to change – this involves reviewing the enablers and barriers that exist that will either help or hinder you in achieving your desired change.

In this section, we will look at your ability to change by considering what levels of willingness and capacity you have at your disposal to enable you to change.

Monique Valcour and John McNulty, experienced and respected business consultants and academics, state in their 2018 *Harvard Business Review* article, 'To Make a Change at Work, Tell Yourself a Different Story', that:

> 'Our brains create coherence by knitting together our internal experience and what we observe in our environment through an automatic process of narrations that explains why we and others do what we do. As we repeat the resulting stories to ourselves (often unconsciously), they become scripts and routines that guide our actions. And instead of recognising our stories for the constructions they are, we may mistakenly interpret them as immutable truths, as the way things are.'

You might think, 'My circumstances correlate to my ability to change. I'm doomed if that's the case.' However, your ability to change is influenced by what you think about your circumstances, not the circumstances themselves.

EXERCISE 2

DETERMINING YOUR ABILITY TO CHANGE

Set aside fifteen minutes and create a list in your journal of your circumstances over the last three months. It might help if you use these three questions as headings:

1. What has persisted over the last three-month period, both good and bad?
2. What has changed for the better over the last three months?
3. What has changed for the worse over the last three months?

Once you have completed this activity, take stock of how you perceive your current circumstances. Do you think you have more ability to change than you first thought, or less?

I have found that by writing a list of my circumstances I have put a boundary around what is occurring and been able to contain it. When I've done this activity, it always seems to make what I'm experiencing that much more manageable. Is that your experience?

> You might think, 'I feel too overwhelmed by my current circumstances,' or 'There's not much I can do about my current circumstances.' Start small and focus on one aspect of your life – work, family, or other relationships. There's no right or wrong here, so start in one area and then progress out.

YOUR WILLINGNESS TO CHANGE

A willingness to change is an openness to accepting something different. Your attitude to change is a key consideration in this instance. Some people love change and others do not. Knowing what your preference is helps with ascertaining your willingness, and whether it needs to be adjusted to enable the change you desire.

This assessment of willingness to change requires an appraisal of how you see your current situation, and how open you are to change. Do you see your current situation as enabling change or limiting change? This is not about who or what has contributed to your current circumstances; rather, it requires you to judge how you see your current circumstances. It's not about being hard on yourself; it's appreciating where you have come to and what might have contributed to that.

A year after I lost my husband, I found that many things around the house needed attention. House maintenance had been my husband's domain and he

1: YOUR STORY IS CALLING YOU

excelled at it. I felt overwhelmed in this situation, so I hesitated to act because of my belief that I lacked the necessary skills to handle the tasks. I discussed this situation with my counsellor, and she helped me see I was in a position where I needed to make adult choices (and not from a position of fear). With this insight, I changed my perspective and did some reflections that completely changed my willingness to act. The tasks were done and done well. I realised I'd learned from my husband and could now put the knowledge to good use. I was willing to act.

By considering your current circumstances, you will gain an indication of your willingness to change. This will help you determine what you consider the degree of difficulty of change to be, and whether you think it's worth it. It also provides an indicator of how you see the likelihood of change taking place.

When I finished school, I didn't get a high enough grade to qualify for university. I eventually entered university at twenty-two, though, as a mature-age student. Many years later, I was considering doing a master's degree, but felt I was not capable enough to do it. It took twenty years of doubting my abilities before I enrolled – then I completed it with a distinction. I was capable of it all along, but was not willing to try simply because of the story I was telling myself about my lack of ability.

You might be thinking, 'I don't think my circumstances are the problem. I'm the problem.' Remember, it is our perception of a situation and the decisions we make because of that perception that are the primary contributors to the circumstances in which we find ourselves. Be mindful not to fall into the global conversations about self-doubt when what you are dealing with is less pervasive and may only require more understanding of where you find yourself.

Anaïs Nin, a French-born American diarist, essayist, and novelist, succinctly sums up what occurs: 'We don't see things as they are. We see them as we are.'

EXERCISE 3

ASSESSING YOUR WILLINGNESS TO CHANGE

Using your journal, and sitting in your favourite location, take ten minutes to list factors in your current circumstances that you think apply to your willingness to change. An example may be: 'I cannot talk to my manager; he does not listen. I need a holiday; I'm so exhausted.'

Prioritise these items on your list based on importance and impact. You might decide to talk to your manager first, to help reduce tension in the workplace. You might also recognise that planning a holiday might take some time. By doing this, you've prioritised the order in which you want to act, and that will help determine your willingness to change and the order in which you choose to change.

You might feel like your current circumstances are insignificant, which prevents you from doing something different. One way to address this is to think of your circumstances as if they're related to someone else. If you were considering the situation at arm's length, what would stand out for you as significant? What is it that makes it significant?

YOUR CAPACITY TO CHANGE – ENABLERS AND BARRIERS

Enablers and barriers affect your situation and provide information about your capacity to change. Enablers are positive resources, skills, and abilities you have. Barriers are any restrictions and deficits that negatively affect your situation. Knowing what these factors are provides information about your capacity to either facilitate change or struggle with it.

These factors can be tangible, such as having enough money in the bank so you can be out of work while you find a new job; and intangible, such as doubting thoughts like, 'I do not think I have what it takes to make the change that I think is needed right now.'

It is important to consider both tangible and intangible factors related to your circumstances.

Enablers can include assets like your home and money in the bank, skills like writing or gardening, and abilities like organising and communicating. Barriers can include lack of sleep, too many commitments, lack of transport, and limited capacity to reflect on one's current situation.

This is not about blaming someone or something else for where you find yourself, or attributing credit for success or good fortune inappropriately. This is like doing a profit and loss statement for where you currently find yourself. What are the assets you can leverage off, and what are the liabilities that might make your circumstances problematic?

An honest appraisal of your enablers and barriers helps determine your current capacity for making the desired and required changes you think necessary at this point. It helps you to know whether you are starting from a positive, neutral, or somewhat negative starting point.

Alasdair Johnson, Frédéric Lefort and Joseph Tesvic state in their McKinsey Report article (2017) that:

> 'The starting point in any strong prioritization process (related to change) is a robust fact base, with a clear understanding of the size and nature of each opportunity, its timing, and any impediments to delivery.'

1: YOUR STORY IS CALLING YOU

This process is best completed when it considers what helps with change, as well as any impediments to the required change that might exist. Taking stock is a key part of the process.

You might try to dispute this by saying, 'I'm not sure about this. I can see plenty of barriers, but few enablers. Does that mean my change is not possible?' If you've determined from the previous sections that you have the ability and willingness to change, these are two enablers that will help combat any of the barriers you may have identified, and positively affect your capacity to change. The likelihood is, you can succeed.

EXERCISE 4

EVALUATING YOUR CAPACITY TO CHANGE

Take out your journal and open it up to a blank double page. This task will take about ten minutes. Pick a location that will allow you to consider your circumstances without interruption. Using the table on the next page as a guide, create your own so you can identify your tangible and intangible enablers (positives) and barriers (negatives).

	ENABLERS	BARRIERS
TANGIBLE		
INTANGIBLE		

Then write as many details as you can in each column to help you explain and define your current circumstances. Once you've done this initial brain dump, walk away.

Come back to this list in three to five days, review it, and add anything that arises that you may not have thought of initially. Rate your circumstances from 0–10, where 0 means 'My circumstances show my capacity to change is low'; 5 means 'My circumstances are okay and I can probably change'; and 10 means 'My circumstances show my capacity to change is high'. This rating will provide you with an objective assessment of how you see your capacity to change.

This exercise allows you to develop a balance sheet of the enablers and barriers likely to affect your ability to act. The initial round focuses on factors above the waterline, so surface-level factors you are already aware of will come to you easily. By then taking the time to walk away and let your brain sit with what you have done for a time, below-the-waterline factors will emerge in the second round. These often-hidden factors will give you the most insight, and contribute to achieving your desired change.

CONCLUSION

In this chapter, you have learned the importance of hearing your own story and understanding it. We then explored this idea by examining your ability, willingness, and capacity to change, because understanding your current situation provides you with valuable data related to these factors.

Now is the time to stop thinking that your story isn't important, and to truly value it. Your story matters. Treat it like a trusted friend who will always have your best interests at heart. It is the starting point to finding what it takes to make the shift you want.

In the next chapter, you will see how your story contributes to a courageous and deliberate step into the unknown, leading you along your next path.

2

MAKING A CHANGE – WHY NOW?

The certainty that comes with knowing why *now* is the right time to act will help power you on. What has happened and what is happening to bring you to this point? This is not about exploring regrets for what you have not done. It is about understanding why you now feel you must do something different, and why what you are doing currently is not sustaining you sufficiently.

It's all in the timing. Why act now and not twenty years ago? Maybe you felt something was not sufficiently in play in your life, like a strong can-do mindset; or you did not feel you had enough resources or support to enable you to make desired changes.

When you understand *why now*, you are more likely to take the actions you desire. It creates a sense of urgency. Otherwise, you risk just going on as you are, and your frustration and discontent will continue and probably grow.

I was forty-eight years old when I came to the realisation that I had a habit of making decisions from a position of fear. Once I saw this, I decided I did not want to continue that way. However, my frustration continued, and I was not sure why. In December 2019, I was reading Susan David's book, *Emotional Agility,* when I had an epiphany – I had to make a conscious choice and take action to no longer be dictated to by fear. I realised there was a big difference between knowing something in my head and changing my behaviour.

It took me thirteen years to get 'knowing' and 'doing' into alignment. Once I did, I made braver decisions, and got to have some wonderful experiences and do things that would not have happened had this change not occurred. Susan David's book was the catalyst that showed me why now was the right time to act. I wanted to live a braver and bolder life, and this was what I needed to do. I'm so glad I made that change because my life is much richer now because of it.

While writing this book, it has been tempting to act from a position of fear, and hold myself back, but if I'm going to live up to my decision, I can't let that define how I approach this project. I need to step up and do it because now is the right time for me to act.

Understanding why now is the time for you to act too will open you up to the adventures that await you as you navigate your next path.

2: MAKING A CHANGE - WHY NOW?

This chapter will help you explore why now is the right time to do something by posing several questions to spark your understanding. The questions explore what has occurred, what you are feeling, and the consequences of taking (or not taking) action.

WHAT HAS OCCURRED?

This question focuses on the tangible circumstances and environmental factors that have occurred for you up to this point in your life, and goes hand in hand with the following one. Take time to consider what has brought you to this point, and enabled you to realise your situation, and choose to do something different. Focus on factors that are occurring for you – for example, a job loss, a serious relationship, a conversation, an illness, or a sick child.

What has occurred is your trigger. You may have ignored jolts in the past, but you're not able to ignore them this time. Don't question why something needs to change. Don't question why this change did not happen earlier. It is about to happen now and you're choosing to respond to it. You're at the point where your present meets your future. This is not about making a resolution. It's about your revolution.

This is the starting point. What has occurred is an undeniable prod for you that you cannot afford to ignore. You must home in on your dissatisfaction with your circumstances as it's causing you to want to do something different. If you don't, you won't know what you want to change.

* * *

Several years ago, Jill was in a role at work that she was finding less satisfying each day, making her feel disheartened and devalued. A contributing factor was Jill's manager, who undermined her and impeded her ability to make a tangible contribution to the organisation's progress. Jill was torn because that job provided her with financial security, and she had built a professional reputation that she could leverage off. Also, Jill was completing a masters of business (MBA) program that her employing organisation was assisting with financially.

Eventually Jill could no longer tolerate what was taking place at work, so she came to me for coaching to help her decide what to do next. Her work environment was starting to affect her physical and mental health, and she realised she could not sustain this in the long term. Jill was also ready to put the learnings from her MBA qualification to good use.

Her coaching time led her to a clear realisation that she needed to do something different, and

2: MAKING A CHANGE – WHY NOW?

with determination, Jill started applying for jobs at a level she had not previously considered. Within two months, Jill secured a more senior role in an organisation more aligned with her values. She was excited to be moving into a position that would enable her to influence the direction of the business, and felt she was contributing meaningfully at work and in society.

* * *

When you know what has occurred in your life to make you want to change, you also know what to change. When you know what to change, you know now is the right time. You might dispute this by saying, 'Nothing specific has occurred. I'm just at the end of my tether.' When you get to a point of saying, 'Enough is enough,' that's usually an indicator it's time to do something different.

EXERCISE 5

DISCERNING WHY NOW IS THE RIGHT TIME TO ACT

Set aside ten minutes with your journal in your preferred location and write down the things that are uppermost in your mind now, in relation to making a change. They don't have to be monumental. Consider those things that are important to you and attract your attention. By doing this, you're articulating factors that are showing why now is the right time to do something. Examples could be, 'I don't like how my manager speaks to me,' 'I find being in a noisy open office distracting, making it hard to get my work done,' or 'I feel like I'm not being heard at home or at work.'

Once you've prepared this list, you're then able to get a greater sense of why the right time to act is now.

However, maybe you aren't sure what has occurred. When I start this exercise by writing just one thing, no matter how small, other things will come to mind, even if my starting point is as simple as, 'My work chair is uncomfortable.' The important thing is that you start with something. Don't think it has to be as big as, say, 'I'm going to change jobs,' or 'I'm going to move to another city.' It can be something small. It could be something like your chair being a problem, or maybe, 'I feel like I need to have a conversation with HR about my future direction.' There are varying degrees of significance in those things, but starting somewhere is the key.

WHAT ARE YOU EXPERIENCING?

This question is equally significant in determining why the right time to act is now. In exercise 5, above, we looked at circumstantial factors that have contributed to your feelings and your need to change. This question is now asking you to consider how you're responding physically, psychologically, and physiologically.

When you sense a need to do something different, your responses to circumstances, more than just the circumstances themselves, are contributing to that feeling. You have more control over your responses to circumstances than you do over the environment, so that is where you can make the most change. By understanding your responses, you gain the information you might need to do things differently to enact the changes you would like to make. This then enables you to successfully level up from the present to the future you desire.

When you can identify the feelings you are experiencing that are intolerable to you, you will know what you need to change to get rid of them.

* * *

Patricia, a long-term casual academic, received an opportunity from the university to become a tenured academic, a permanent position that was scarce. Her biggest challenges when considering this offer were how she felt about this and how she perceived herself.

Because she'd been a casual academic for a long time, she felt she would probably never get a tenured position, and she also struggled with feeling she may not be good enough for the role. Old paradigms, both personal and external, were no longer of benefit to Patricia.

Our first coaching session together set in motion a process that is continuously changing even after two years. Through exploring her feelings about her current situation, and knowing which feelings were causing her discomfort, she was able to determine why *now* was the right time to act. By taking the time to explain her feelings, Patricia completely changed how she presented herself, not only in interviews but in all her interactions. She continues to show up and be the capable, credible academic that she's always hoped to be, but had struggled to picture for herself.

* * *

2: MAKING A CHANGE – WHY NOW?

Patricia's story shows that when you can identify the cause of the discomfort you are feeling, this pinpoints not only why now is the right time to act but also what you need to act on.

Please note: When I ask you to complete exercises that require you to access another website, be assured that I'm sending you to reputable sites where experts have tested the available tools and found them to be valuable and reliable; and where most of the time you can access those tools for free.

EXERCISE 6

REVIEWING FEELINGS

You might dispute the use of this activity by saying, 'I don't know how I feel. It's been ages since I thought about it.' If so, find a list of a range of feelings, either online or in a book to prompt you.

(The Hoffman Institute offers a comprehensive list called 'Practices, Feelings, Sensations' on their website: www.hoffmaninstitute.org/wp-content/uploads/Practices-FeelingsSensations.pdf)

At the end of each day, for ten days, tick the words that best apply to the feelings you've experienced

> that day. Place a tick next to the pleasant ones and a cross next to the unpleasant ones. At the end of ten days, see if any patterns are emerging in the feelings you've marked, both pleasant and unpleasant. This will provide you with information on the feelings you would like more of, and those that may contribute to your discomfort. Once you have completed this exercise, include it in your journal.

One barrier that can arise with this exercise is finding it difficult to allow yourself to feel vulnerable. In the April 2023 edition of *Psychology Today*, Dr Tchiki Davis stated in her article, 'The Benefits of Vulnerability', that there are three key benefits of allowing ourselves to be vulnerable:

1. It can ease anxiety.
2. It can strengthen relationships.
3. It can help you become more self-aware.

She says that learning to label your emotions in simple ways, and journaling, help develop your ability to be vulnerable. Take a risk.

If you're already feeling discomfort, acknowledging the discomfort is the first step to allowing yourself to be vulnerable. Recognise that there are benefits in this. It's not a sign of weakness. It's a sign of strength and it will help you discern why the right time to act is now.

WHAT IS THE CONSEQUENCE OF DOING SOMETHING?

Doing something is the point where you've decided that now is the time to act. It's not tomorrow or next week, it's right now. (In the next section we will look at the consequences of not acting.)

When deciding to act, there are two parts to this consideration:

1. What will happen if you do? How will things change, and what might you gain as a result? For example, you may need to change the organisation you work for, which will give you a chance to apply your skills and learn.
2. What won't happen if you do? This is the opportunity cost of acting. What will you need to forego? For example, you will not get the promotion that has come up in your current organisation if you take a new role elsewhere.

When you understand the risks of actions, you are likely to act and not doubt your choices after you do. Think back to Jill's story, where she expressed discontent with her current situation at work. It was causing her stress and affecting her mental health, so she knew she had to change. The consequence for Jill was leaving the organisation she knew well, and starting over elsewhere. The outcome for Jill was to begin working for an organisation that was more closely aligned with her values and moving in the direction she wanted to take in her life.

Pinpointing that *now* is the time to do something different in your life places you in an excellent position to know where to start, which we will discuss in more detail in the next chapter. Doing something is not always easy, though, as you may experience more discomfort initially.

However, if you have considered all the things we've discussed to this point in the book, you will have an awareness of the consequences of acting, and you will have decided that doing something is the right action for you to take to progress along your next path. This was the result in Jill's case, and it can be for you, too. Jill stepped out of her comfort zone to act. It took bravery and commitment. But, as Jill discovered, it was worth it.

If one of the challenges you have with this concept is to imagine a consequence, think about one thing that will change if you do something different. It could be as simple as, 'I will have to take an earlier train to work if I change jobs.' What might occur that is likely to take you out of your current comfort zone? Which of your current everyday habits would be impacted if you decided now was the right time to change?

2: MAKING A CHANGE – WHY NOW?

EXERCISE 7

FEATURES OF DESIRED CHANGE

Return to your comfortable location with your journal. Spend fifteen minutes starting a list, and on your first attempt, write as many potential positive results that would result from your desired change. Write a minimum of three – and as many as you can.

Then list as many things as you can that you might have to forgo because of this change. Ideas and thoughts might come quickly initially and then slow down. Sit with the quiet and see what else might come to mind. Write at least three.

You might find that you have other ideas later. If the opportunity arises, add to your list as other thoughts crop up. Sometimes our minds need time to sit with things and then ideas will come to light. The initial activity puts the ideas into your head, and you are now guiding your thoughts rather than just operating uncontrolled or on remote control.

You might think, 'I just can't think of any consequences.' Do not overcomplicate what might be a consequence. It does not have to be something monumental. It can be small, like, 'I will have to go to a different platform to get the train to work if I change jobs.'

WHAT IS THE CONSEQUENCE OF DOING NOTHING?

You might make a conscious choice to do nothing to change your current situation. You just decide to continue the status quo. This is different from the cost associated with doing something where we must forego something else because we cannot do everything. Doing nothing means you're going to let things stay exactly as they are and live with it. Some call this the line of least resistance – you do what you consider to be the easiest thing – but it's not necessarily the right choice. You choose to stay in your comfort zone, even though it may be uncomfortable.

The discomfort you feel is familiar and you may be reluctant to go into an unfamiliar space. But it's flawed logic. There can be both benefits and risks to doing nothing. When you know what they are, you have at least made a conscious choice, which might make it all feel better. Inaction is a choice. We might think there are no consequences to this choice, but there are.

After my husband had passed away and I was alone, the kitchen-sink tap broke, and I didn't have hot water in my kitchen for several months. I decided not to do anything about it because I felt I was dealing with bigger life challenges, and it could wait. I chose not to act. However, the inconvenience and frustration I felt because of not fixing this tap grew and grew until it got to a point where

2: MAKING A CHANGE – WHY NOW?

I became constantly aggravated. I eventually got my kitchen tap fixed after three to four months of inconvenience and I could not believe the relief I felt once it was done. Yet it was only a kitchen tap.

My choice not to act at that time seemed like a good idea for my overall sense of wellbeing, at one level, but it was not. I took a short-sighted view of the implications of not having a kitchen tap. This, unfortunately, is also the case with bigger decisions we need to make. While not acting seems like a good idea in the moment, that is not usually how it pans out in the long run.

You might say, 'The consequence of doing nothing is only insignificant.' There are usually many unforeseen consequences of not acting and most will eventually, if left long enough, affect your health and wellbeing. They will cause an irritation that typically only increases until we attend to it.

EXERCISE 8

CONSEQUENCES OF CHOOSING NOT TO ACT

It's time to revisit your journal. Take ten minutes in your preferred location and think about a time when you chose not to act. It could have been as simple as choosing not to go out with your friends on a Friday night. When you reflect on that instance,

> determine whether you think choosing not to act was a wise or unwise decision. What made it wise or unwise? For example, 'Not going out with friends was a good idea as it meant I did not wake up with a hangover on Saturday morning,' or 'It was an unwise idea because by not going out with friends, I missed out on a big announcement by one of them, so I wasn't there to share it with them, which left me disappointed.'
>
> We typically understand things in hindsight, so I am asking you to reflect on an experience where you can now consider the consequences or impact of not acting.

When we think about taking a course of action, we will have some form of reaction, ranging from excitement to fear and varying states in between. Consider how you are reacting and how this is impacting your decision to act or not. If something changes for you, would it increase the likelihood of you acting? If so, why, and what can you do to make this happen?

2: MAKING A CHANGE - WHY NOW?

CONCLUSION

We've looked at why discovering *now* is the right time to act is important by answering four key questions:

1. What has occurred that means now is the right time to do something?
2. What are you experiencing that has led you to this point where now is the right time to act?
3. What is the consequence of doing something?
4. What is the consequence of doing nothing?

These questions are powerful as they help you determine whether *now* is the right time to act and take those initial steps along your next path.

By working through these questions, you will consider your current circumstances and feelings, and the consequences of action and inaction. This information will empower you to then determine where you want to start, which we will discuss in the next chapter.

Stop finding excuses that are simply aversion strategies to encourage you to stay in your comfort zone. Start thinking about what will be different for you if you choose to do something new that extends your comfort zone. You cannot do everything, but you can do something.

3

START HERE

Now that you have spent some time listening to yourself and getting clear and current with your story today (not who you were ten years ago), and you understand why now is the right time to act, let's look at where to start, so you can level up your life and make the shift you want.

You cannot do everything. Identifying a place to start is a critical first step. It helps you put a stake in the ground and orients you in the direction you wish to go. We are not talking about the destination at this point. We are focusing on the starting point. The ideas explored in this chapter will help you determine where yours is. By reviewing the meaning and merit of starting at any point, you can accomplish this. You will also identify anything else you need to consider, which will help you determine the suitability of the starting point you identify.

LIFE'S NEXT PATH

At age fifty, I was considering a change of career. I'd been in an accounting-related role in my early career, progressing into process, project, and quality-management roles within a large corporate organisation. I had become restless and knew I wanted to do something else.

People had frequently suggested that I would make a good counsellor, but in my mind, that was way beyond me. Coincidentally, at that time my local church was about to run an Introduction to Pastoral Counselling course over four weeks. I decided this would be a good place to start. It did not require extensive time or financial commitments, and it would give me a taste of counselling so I could better decide whether this was what I wanted to do. I could also back out with little consequence if it turned out that it didn't measure up to what I thought it would be.

If you don't zero in on your starting point, there are two big risks. First, you'll feel overwhelmed and dissatisfied. My short course meant there was less chance I would feel overwhelmed by a big change, and if I felt dissatisfied, I could back out easily. Second, you will meander around and procrastinate, increasing the likelihood that you'll do nothing. Again, by finding a starting point, I at least had my nose pointed in the direction I was considering.

* * *

3: START HERE

Leanne was working in a large international corporation with a manager who took every opportunity to undermine her. Despite her capabilities, she felt stuck where she was. She loved the work she was doing and the people she served. She knew she needed to make a shift, and yet she could not specify a place to start. This led to her eventually taking time off, as she became unwell and needed time to recover. Unfortunately, this left long-term scars that drastically affected her confidence. It caused her to freeze, and she stagnated for a long time.

Unfortunately, Leanne's story is not a one-off thing. Without taking the time to find what you want and where to start, there are risk implications that have drastic long-term effects. Starting somewhere is less risky than starting nowhere.

* * *

Let's now look at four essential ideas in sequence. These activities happen in unison, but for explanation, I have separated them. The four ideas are:

1. Start with the doable. Acknowledge the scope of the changes you are contemplating, then determine what is doable and where a valid starting point might be for you.
2. Determine what is meaningful. By doing this, you ensure you direct your efforts and energies effectively.
3. Get the most from your efforts. Review the merit of the starting point you have

identified to ensure it is the best place to direct your efforts and energies.
4. Identify other considerations. Review other factors to ensure you make an effective and thoughtful decision about a starting point. Don't overlook any key aspects that might derail your progress.

You can refer to the barriers and enablers you identified in Chapter 1 to assist you in determining where you start. For example, if one of your options in your next path includes a promotion in your existing field, that is a different challenge to changing careers altogether, from, say, public service to architecture. While becoming an architect is doable, even if you are sixty-three, it will be an enormous challenge because of the years of study and the industry requirements.

WHAT IS DOABLE?

Acknowledge the scope of the changes you are contemplating, then determine what is doable and where a valid starting point might be for you. There are four keywords in that statement:

1. Acknowledge: Recognise the importance or significance of what you are considering.
2. Scope: This is the depth, breadth, and width of the opportunity or possibility that you're considering.

3. Doable: Is it within your circumstances and abilities to do this?
4. Valid: Assess whether this is a legitimate place for you to start.

Remember, this is not about judging the validity of the starting point. It is the identification of it. This activity is about recognising what you want to do, the extent of what is involved in doing it, and whether it's doable given your current circumstances. In other words, is this a legitimate place to start? (Later in this chapter, you will look at suitability when assessing the merit of your starting point.)

As with the architect example, is starting from scratch in an industry with stringent professional standards what you want to do if you are sixty-three? The answer might be yes, but it is also worth considering if there is an alternative that could be equally fulfilling, therefore making what you want and what you are aiming for realistic. You can dream big and do anything, but you need to know what you are in for.

Most things in life do not start in the middle. They start at the beginning, and this beginning has usually been determined through thought and review. I know that when I set out to write this book, the first things I needed to do were acknowledge an appropriate scope, determine what was doable, and pinpoint where I might start, especially when the temptation to write 'everything' in a book can be strong. It was scary to narrow my choices, but I needed to do it, so I had a clearly defined starting point for my book.

An integral part of that was determining who would be most interested in reading what I wrote.

The process of writing a book has many parallels with other actions in our lives – choosing our goal, recognising our capacity, and identifying where to start. However, when it comes to change in your life, you might be thinking, 'I have too much going on. How am I going to determine the starting point? It's all too confusing.' The good news is that you do not have to start with the ultimate destination in mind. You can start with one step on the path you want to go on.

I started on the path to writing this book by deciding who I would like to read it, not what the entire book was about. That was a step in the direction I wanted to go. If you're unsure of where to begin, or if it feels overwhelming, picture yourself untangling a piece of string. Find an end of that string to begin, then each action you take will help the untangling process. Start somewhere.

You might also wonder, 'How will I know whether what I want is doable?' In the very early stages of change, you will probably make an educated guess. When I attended the pastoral counselling course, I had no idea what I would learn from it. I didn't even know what pastoral counselling was – but it had the word counselling in it, so I thought I might learn something relevant. As it turned out, I did. Pastoral counselling is counselling that's focused on psychological and emotional aspects of a person's life, as well as issues of faith and ethics.

EXERCISE 9

STEPS FOR MAKING CHANGE

Go back to your journal and set yourself up in your favourite location. Take thirty minutes to complete this activity. Think about a minor change you would like to make, for example, including more movement in your day. Consider the following seven points:

1. Define what movement would mean for you – walking, running, upper-body movement, swimming, arm stretches, or something else.
2. Which would you find the easiest of those options, and why?
3. Which would you find the hardest, and why?
4. Determine how much time each day you would give to each one that you've chosen.
5. Decide if it's something you would do every day or only a certain number of times per week.
6. What would need to happen to make this possible?
7. What would prohibit this happening?

After considering these factors, how doable do you think adding more movement into your day would be?

Apply these same steps to any change you're considering. Think about two or three aspects of your current circumstance you identified in the previous chapter and use one of those as your starting point. Start small. This is not about taking on something monumental. It is always about baby steps.

Then go through the seven questions again in relation to what you are considering doing:

1. Define what it would mean if you did what you're considering.
2. What would you find easiest?
3. What might you find hardest?
4. How long might you need to do it each day?
5. Is it something you want to do every day, once a week or once a month?
6. What would need to take place to make it possible?
7. What could prohibit it from happening?

If you take these steps, you will better understand what is required. Starting small is enough. Ultimately this is about determining what is doable.

FIND A STARTING POINT

Determine a meaningful starting point to ensure your efforts and energies are well-directed. It must be something important and worthwhile to you, and get you up in the morning.

We all have limited amounts of energy to devote to what we want to do in our lives, and ideally we direct those energies in constructive and purposeful ways. Let's now look at the best place for you to start.

Part of what drove me to study counselling was the motto I live by – pay it forward. Because I have been fortunate enough to have good mentors and guides in my life, I believe I have a responsibility to pay that forward to others. Learning to counsel meant I would have the skills that would enable me to help others more effectively.

This is not about trying to find the best place to start or the best criteria to use to determine where you start along your next path – this is about finding *a* starting point.

Some may have thought my best place to start would have been a full counselling course, but the partial course gave me a taster, so I didn't feel out of my depth and become dissuaded from continuing. It helped me to see that it was meaningful to me, and doable. For you, starting something meaningful and doable will mean you are exerting your energies to take you in the direction you want to go. We might all be working out how to travel our next path and yet we will all come to it from a different direction.

If you choose something meaningful, you are likely to enjoy it, whether it leads to your goal or not. You want it to connect with your head and heart.

Have you ever been out driving and taken a wrong turn? You then had to take time to do a route recalculation via a U-turn or a diversion you were not expecting. Metaphorical wrong turns can happen at the start of your journey as well as along your next path.

Many years ago, when I was going to a close friend's mother's funeral, I missed a turn and could not find my way, causing me to miss the service. I felt I had let my friend down in a big way. My intention was to be there and support my friend, as that meant a lot to me. But sometimes, we cannot help but take a wrong turn in life and so we need to regroup and set ourselves up to start again.

If you ensure that your starting point holds meaning for you, you can reduce the risk of taking that wrong turn and getting diverted from what you consider important and worthwhile.

Maybe you're thinking, 'I do not know what has meaning for me anymore.' If that is you, think about an activity that brought you joy in the past. What was it about that activity that made it joyful? Your responses will help highlight what has meaning for you.

It doesn't have to be anything earth-shattering. It could be something that simply makes you smile, like sitting in a swing at a park, or seeing a dog. Then ask yourself what it is about animals that causes you to smile, specifically dogs. Or swings. There may be something in your responses that tells you what gives you meaning. Take time to explore what that might be.

If you are an avid risk-taker and you like the thrill of the chase, keep taking risks if you think they're worth it. But take risks that align with what has meaning for you, not just risks for the sake of taking risks.

EXERCISE 10

DETERMINING A MEANINGFUL STARTING POINT

Take fifteen minutes in your favourite place to think about what a meaningful starting point might look like, which can include considerations such as:

- What fills you with energy?
- What makes you feel happy?
- What types of people do you like to spend time with?
- What happens on days when you feel fulfilled?
- What causes you to feel satisfied?
- What makes you feel proud of yourself?

Take the time to consider these things. Write your thoughts in your journal and answer each of these questions in as much depth as you can. The more depth you add to your responses, the more you will see why the starting point you identify will be a meaningful one.

Are you still struggling to identify what gives you meaning? If you're not sure what makes you happy, start small. What gives you a sense of contentment? For example, time with your family, your friends, or going to a particular holiday location. Consider what you like about those times. This will give you a glimpse of what matters to you.

I found meaning down by the river – it gives me a sense of serenity. I want to ensure that wherever I start and whatever I do, calmness and peace of mind will always be a part of it. If that is not there at the actual starting point, I will always ensure that the actions I take will lead me to a place of tranquillity.

DETERMINE THE MERIT OF YOUR STARTING POINT

Review the merit – the worthwhile qualities – of your starting point to ensure its suitability and that it is taking you in the direction where you are happy to exert your efforts and energies. This is another time to review your actions. The key point here is to confirm you are facing in the direction you want to go, be it north, south, east, or west. It's about following the best option for you.

This is like a mini cost-benefit analysis, specifically at the starting point. Consider what you gain (by starting at the identified starting point) and what you might lose or forego (cost) by having this as your starting point. With my pastoral counselling course, I gained insight and other benefits from learning more about the role of a counsellor, while the cost was giving up four evenings to attend the course, which meant I could not use that time for something else. Did I consider it meaningful to do that? In this instance, yes.

Remember, we are looking here at the merit of the starting point, not the merit of the entire journey. If you have determined you want to start your journey facing east, consider why beginning in the east is the most suitable direction, as opposed to the west, north, or south. You must choose a starting point that you consider important and advantageous. If you want to be a CEO, for example, does starting as a cleaner align with what you consider to be beneficial? Does it have merit, from your perspective?

Jill, who you met in Chapter 2, had determined that her starting point was to take her business course to give her knowledge and skills that would help her stand out for more senior roles. Through analysis, she had realised that maintaining the status quo would not give her the leverage she needed. She determined that having influential status within an organisation where she could help shape strategy was important to her. Self-development had meaning for her, so starting with the MBA was important, both personally and professionally. In Jill's case, this starting point had merit, and she concentrated her efforts on travelling her next path.

You might be thinking, 'I'm not even sure what I think is important or worthwhile to me anymore.' If that sounds like you, think about the last time you had to make a big decision of some kind. You had to start somewhere.

How do you typically start your decision-making processes, especially when significant choices need to be made? What of that process could you apply in this case to help you determine what you consider to be consequential? Start with one thing and expand from there.

EXERCISE 11

REVIEWING ENABLERS AND BARRIERS

Returning to your journal, take 15–30 minutes to review what you did in your exercise on enablers and barriers in Chapter 2. Identify what you consider important and worthwhile, and what you are willing to invest in to harness the enablers and overcome the barriers. Then take time to think about what new insights this may have brought to light for you. Are there any changes you think you might need to make? Is there anything you might need to delete? Take these discoveries and use them to help you assess the merit of your starting point.

What if you are not able to see the merit of your starting point? Could it be that you're trying to see more than you need to? Narrow the scope of what you are looking for. Remember the KISS principle here – keep it simple and straightforward. Don't over-complicate it, as this will help you identify the things that make this a meritorious starting point.

WHAT ELSE DO YOU NEED TO THINK ABOUT?

Identify anything else you need to consider so you can enable effective and thoughtful determination of a starting point. Ensure that you do not overlook any key aspects that might take you off track. This is where you can bring together all of your insights from Chapters 2 and 3 so far.

This is your sanity check regarding your starting point. Let's talk again about the 63-year-old man who wants to become an architect: he could do it. He feels it's meaningful and valuable, but even if he invested in five years of study to become qualified, he may still not get a job in the industry as there are professional standards he would need to meet, which could take another three years. He may, based on that, determine it's not a valid starting point. It's doable and meets some other criteria, but the merit of it at this point in his life is probably not as high as it needs to be.

In the last two chapters, you've given serious consideration to your starting point. Now is the time to take these insights and bring them together as an integrated whole. This is the section about your sanity check. Have you applied sound reasoning, and is there anything missing? Things can be doable, meaningful, and valuable and still not make sense.

* * *

Kiran had a lot going on in her life. She was about to lose her job. Her children were getting ready to leave the nest and her relationship with her husband was strained. She had many potential starting points she could have acted from. We talked through the dilemmas in her life, and she undertook the starting point review as outlined in Chapters 2 and 3.

She considered what would change if she worked on changing her job situation, what could change if she worked on the relationship with her husband, and what would change if she adjusted how she was responding to her children leaving the nest.

What Kiran found most actionable and purposeful was working on her own self-worth, as she knew it would have positive implications for her personally and professionally. The analysis showed that it would give her the greatest flow-on effect. This gave it the highest rating for 'doable, meaningful, and valuable', showing that it had the most merit as a starting point for her. Because she started there and worked forward, other aspects of her life also improved. Her communication with her family members was more caring and considerate.

* * *

> Most decisions involve choice. One way to make wise choices is to use the 'doable, meaningful, and valuable' criteria. By doing so, Kiran maximised the benefits she gained because she made an informed assessment of her starting point and its relative merit.

> Could she have started anywhere? Absolutely, with no question. Ideally, find your optimal starting point and work from there. Remember, it is not about what's 'best', because best is undefinable. It's about your optimal choice, having done the homework.

You might ask, 'How can I know if my decision regarding my starting point makes sense?' The reality is that maybe you cannot be sure, but most of us can trust our common sense, and personal and professional experience over many, many years.

EXERCISE 12

CRITICAL REVIEW OF STARTING POINT

Return to your journal and set aside fifteen minutes for this task in your preferred location, where you won't face any interruptions. Write down what you've determined your starting point to be. Consider if you have used sound reasoning – applying logical and critical thinking – to identify your starting point. What makes it sound reasoning? Consider what would make this an appropriate starting point. Be unrestrained in your thinking about this.

In doing this review, does this help you confirm this is a valid starting point, or cause you to question what

> you've decided to do? Has this analysis helped you to identify anything that is missing? If so, go back and add this to what you have identified as your starting point. Remember, this activity will enable you to do a final sanity check, identifying your start-here point – because that's what this chapter is about: Start here!

CONCLUSION

In this chapter, you've discovered how to identify what you want to start with by considering three things:

1. The starting point you've identified as doable by defining its scope
2. Identifying whether the starting point is for you because you consider it important and worthwhile
3. Investigating the suitability or merit of that starting point

You concluded the exploration with a sanity check of your starting point by applying logical and critical thinking to determine its suitability. It may seem to be on a small scale – and you need to stop procrastinating. Determining the validity of your starting point is critical, so the only thing to do is get started.

In the next chapter, things will get interesting. I will help you learn the importance of hearing your own voice, and how to slay the saboteurs so you will make the right choices for yourself.

SLAYING THE SABOTEURS

As we approach change, whether we choose it or it is forced upon us, we inevitably have to deal with our own stirred-up emotions, thoughts, and opinions, some encouraging and some not so much. It's time now to learn how to trust and listen to your own voice, and slay the saboteurs within.

Who you are now is not who you were twenty, ten, or even five years ago. Let's review and update your understanding of you.

As a positive-psychology practitioner, I always advocate starting from a position of strength rather than focusing only on the problem or circumstance that requires attention. For that reason, let's dive into your values, beliefs, belief systems, and strengths, because that powerful toolkit will guide your actions and provide methods for combating saboteurs.

It's helpful to think of this concept as a sandwich. Your values, beliefs, belief systems, and strengths make up the bottom slice of bread, the foundation, while what gives you meaning, purpose and inspiration makes up the top slice of bread. The saboteurs are the sandwich filling. The slices of bread keep the filling contained so it doesn't fall out everywhere and make a mess that you then need to clean up.

This chapter focuses on you hearing and learning what matters to you by exploring and identifying factors that help define you and what you stand for now. It's all about hearing your voice with no disruptions from external noise, whether it be other people's opinions, or the expectations you have for yourself. You will consider your values, beliefs and belief systems, and your strengths, while identifying any saboteurs that hinder you from moving forward as you would like to. This is about staying true to yourself and not being swayed by others, whereas Chapter 1 was about hearing your own story.

These explorations and investigations help you understand what provides you with meaning and purpose. They also help you see how you honour yourself and the value you place on your pursuits, and how you position yourself in important relationships. When you understand all these things and their relevance for you, you'll be in a much better position to slay your saboteurs.

Learning what makes us who we are and what makes us tick is something we rarely take time to do. In her book, *The Gifts of Imperfection*, Brené Brown, the international author and thought leader, says that living incongruently is exhausting.

Derek Rydall, spiritual life coach and author of *Emergence: Seven Steps for Radical Life Change* (2015), calls it a crisis in his article, 'The Crisis of Incongruence', in *The Huffington Post* in August 2017. He stated that living with internal conflict is fatiguing, and a hidden cause of unhappiness. In his book, he built his argument that the answers you seek are already inside you:

> 'We can't heal what we don't feel. We can't have a future until we fully inhabit our present. It's like the proverbial Groundhog Day. Most people don't live 70–90 years; they live the same year 70–90 times because they keep regurgitating an incomplete present.'

How do you get rid of internal conflict? You must understand what drives you and gives your life meaning and purpose – your values, belief systems, and strengths – and recognise the saboteurs and negative voices that try to take you off course. Honouring your pursuits, yourself, and your relationships is important because they affect the value you place on yourself and what you want and need in life.

VALUES AND BELIEFS (ENABLING AND LIMITING)

Consider your values and beliefs (enabling and limiting) and belief systems to determine what matters to you, and how they influence how you think and act. These are tools you have available to slay your saboteurs.

Values are the personal traits you believe are important to the way you live, like honesty and kindness, and define who you are and who you would like to be. Across a wide range of situations, they help guide you to make optimal choices. They are your compass. They will always point you toward your true north. If a saboteur suggests you go a different way, you can offer a counter view to dismiss their input and reduce their impact.

Beliefs are things you accept as being true and correct. They do not have to be based on fact. They can be opinions or assumptions. There are three different types of beliefs that someone can have:

1. Fact: e.g. the earth is round
2. An opinion that may be examined, e.g. democracy is better than socialism
3. Assumption, often unfounded, e.g. a belief in the afterlife, or fairies or ghosts

Enabling beliefs are those that inspire you. For example, in my case, 'I can write a book.' Limiting beliefs are those that hold you back. An example in my case would be, 'I am not a good writer.'

4: SLAYING THE SABOTEURS

Belief systems are tenets or ideas that people have formed over time. They often fall into categories such as political, spiritual or religious, societal, and philosophical, e.g. Buddhists, socialists, humanists, or collectivists. The term 'worldview' often includes someone's beliefs and belief systems.

You have chosen your values, beliefs, and belief systems, and they help determine the tone and modulation of your internal voice. Understanding how you speak, not just what you say, and recognising what causes your internal voice to become loud or soft, fast or slow, are all important when hearing your voice.

Your voice is the primary tool you have to slay the saboteurs. I know that when I'm excited, or associated with something I believe in or value, I talk faster, and my voice goes up. However, when I'm angry, or when something I value is being undervalued or compromised, the same thing happens, and yet the impact is quite different. This is all important information, and knowing which is which helps to moderate your actions and inform decisions you need to make.

Most people would not travel today without a GPS or a Google map. Values and beliefs are like maps, ensuring you're heading in the direction you want to take. Several years ago, I felt like I'd gone off course. I soon realised it had been a long time since I'd last revisited my values, so I sat down with my journal and opened to where I had last captured them. I wanted to extend how I had documented them, so I created a mind map and included where I wanted to focus on the specific values I had identified. While I did this in 2022, it still guides me today, and I take time to review it regularly to ensure that it still holds enough relevance and guidance for me today.

I identified my six core values as authenticity, credibility, role modelling, personal evolution, pay-it-forward mentality, and offering a compelling point of view; and each one opened up to reveal the sub-values that had importance for me, as summarised in the table below.

Carol's Values

VALUE	SUB-VALUES
Credible	Believable
	Dependable
	Plausible
Compelling	Evoking interest, attention, and admiration
	Enthralling
	Persuasive
	Well-reasoned
Personal evolution	Voluntarily undertaken
	Lifelong learning
	Learning to know, do and be
Pay it forward	Paid
	Unpaid

4: SLAYING THE SABOTEURS

VALUE	SUB-VALUES
Role modelling	Family
	Friends
	Clients
	Colleagues
Authenticity	Person of conviction
	Real
	Truthful

These values have a significant influence on, and interrelationship with, my beliefs and belief systems, and together they act as a lighthouse, keeping me focused on my chosen direction and reducing the chances of becoming shipwrecked.

If you ignore your values, beliefs, and belief systems, then being equipped to face challenges, also known as saboteurs, becomes much more difficult. It is like you are ignoring the valuable tools you have in your toolkit, which just makes little or no sense.

What if you feel you don't know what your values are? I had a conversation with a client about this recently, as he had never taken the time to identify his beliefs and ideals. After he thought about what they were, he identified one or two and it was like someone had switched a light on for him. Values are the light in the lighthouse that helps guide you, and they help inform what you do.

LIFE'S NEXT PATH

EXERCISE 13A

IDENTIFYING YOUR VALUES

Take thirty minutes to complete the Values Assessment Worksheet referenced on the following page. You will rate each listed value on a scale of 1–10, where 1 is not significant at all to you, 5 is moderately significant to you, and 10 is critical to you.

Use the first fifteen minutes to complete the worksheet. Then, use the next fifteen minutes to review your responses and how you feel about completing this process.

List the top three values you've identified as being most important to you – three that you have rated 9 or 10. Now consider how these values affect what you do. Think about how you might have applied them over the last month. What impact did they have on what you did? Were you aware of this at the time?

Starting with values helps you learn more about, and connect to, your beliefs and belief systems. How do you think they're interconnected?

Values Assessment Worksheet: If you go to the following link you will find a worksheet that will enable you to consider your values and come up with a list that has meaning for you:

www.thewellnesssociety.org/wp-content/uploads/2022/11/Values-Worksheets.pdf

This is a comprehensive worksheet that allows you to list not only your values but also how you intend to live out those values in everyday life.

EXERCISE 13B

IDENTIFYING YOUR BELIEFS

Beliefs Assessment Worksheet: At the following link you will find a List of Generic Negative and Positive Beliefs:

www.emdrtherapyvolusia.com/wp-content/uploads/2016/12/Beliefs_Negative_Positive.pdf

It is important to remember that beliefs do come in two forms: they are enabling (I can) and limiting (I can't). As a further exercise, should you choose to do it, complete the beliefs worksheet that follows by taking these three steps:

1. Using the list provided on the website (above link), identify the beliefs you hold, both positive and negative.
2. Note whether you think each belief you have selected is an enabling belief or a limiting belief.
3. Identify your top three enabling beliefs and your top three limiting beliefs.

Try not to judge the beliefs you identify in this exercise. Just ask yourself how they are informing the actions you take, and how they can help equip you to do the things you would like to do. Can you identify what might get in your way?

You might ask, 'How do I decide which value is more important than another?' Think of someone you admire. What quality or qualities do you admire in them? Do you think you have that quality? If so, do you think it's beneficial? Is it a quality that you think influences what you do and how you interact with others?

Referring to my sandwich analogy earlier in this chapter, you've now identified the foundation piece because you now understand your values and beliefs. Both values and beliefs will inform your belief system. Understanding your belief system

4: SLAYING THE SABOTEURS

> will develop from doing this exploration. Later in the chapter, we will look at what gives you meaning and purpose, and where you find inspiration and interaction, which is the top of your sandwich.

STRENGTHS AND HOW TO LEVERAGE THEM

Knowing your own strengths means determining the personal resources you have to draw from that will take you where you want to go. They are your character traits, skills, or abilities you consider positive, and can include knowledge, attributes, and talents.

I want you to hear your own voice here, and recognise the strengths you believe you have – not something someone else tells you they see in you.

Some of my strengths include mental arithmetic, pattern recognition in numbers and words, empathy, and getting to the kernel of an issue. My clients have a wide range of strengths, like outstanding sales skills, presentation skills, and optimistic viewpoints.

Strengths can be grouped in many ways. One option is to group them into the following four categories – interpersonal, intellectual, emotional, and restraint – and the following table gives an example of each. This is not an exhaustive list of strengths, just examples of types in each category. If you think of other strengths you have, I encourage you to include them in a list you make for yourself. Use the information in the table as the starting point for building a table of your own strengths, grouped into these four categories.

Types of Skills/Strengths by Category

INTERPERSONAL STRENGTHS	INTELLECTUAL STRENGTHS
• Communication • Empathy • Active listening • Collaboration	• Creativity • Extensive vocabulary • Problem-solving • Mathematical abilities • Understanding physics
EMOTIONAL STRENGTHS	RESTRAINT STRENGTHS
• Resilience • Compassion • Ability to be vulnerable • Perseverance • Hopefulness	• Knowing when to act and when to hold back • An ability to restrain and contain anger • Responding, not reacting

Understanding and identifying your strengths gives you data about the tools available to you when you undertake your personal do-it-yourself (DIY) project. You would never do a practical DIY project without checking what tools you already have, and assessing whether you need to update your toolkit – and this is no different.

According to a study conducted by Brian Brim, a senior practice partner for Gallup, the well-known research organisation, putting a focus on strengths can improve several things. The study showed there were higher levels of engagement at work and individuals also had higher levels of wellbeing. For more information on the results of this study go to:

www.gallup.com/workplace/242096/focus-people-strengths-increases-work-engagement.aspx

I first came across the idea of adopting a strengths-based approach in 2010, when I was in the last year of my master's degree at that time. I came across the VIA Institute on Character based in Ohio, USA, and undertook their Values in Action (VIA) signature strengths assessment.

I was pleased and surprised to find out what my signature strengths were, particularly when my top intellectual strength showed as love of learning. Given that I call myself a learning addict, this made me happy. It was also validation of the importance I placed on learning. It was something that had consistently informed what I have done – and still does to this day. I also discovered that my weakest character strength was humour, which, ironically, made me laugh.

While I might have predicted some results, seeing my strongest strengths listed in order was like honing the tools of my toolkit. I then knew which were sharp and which were not. This process also highlighted strengths I never knew I had, which meant I had tools in my toolkit that I was not even aware of. Being aware of their existence put me in a better position to learn how to use them effectively.

There is much to be gained by understanding your current strengths because that insight can also help you apply what you learn in this chapter. You might be thinking, 'I've got this far in life already. Do I really need to look at my strengths now?' If you are desiring to make a change, knowing what you have at hand to help facilitate that process can only benefit you in the long run.

Because you are reading this book, I suspect you are seeking to do something different, and gaining awareness of your current strengths (both expected and unexpected) will only help you do that.

EXERCISE 14

IDENTIFYING YOUR SIGNATURE STRENGTHS

For this exercise, I ask you to complete your free Values in Action (VIA) signature strength assessment at this website: www.viacharacter.org/account/register.

Register first, so you can have your survey results returned to you. The assessment will probably take you 10–15 minutes to complete, then the website will send you a report outlining your signature strengths. (You can always unsubscribe from the site once you have your report.)

I advise you to complete the next step within an hour of receiving your report, so your experience is fresh in your mind.

Once you receive your report, return to your journal. Think about the results of the process, and what it was like answering the questions as you completed the assessment. The results are important, but so are your experiences as you completed the task. Answer the following questions in your journal:

- Was there anything in the report you agreed with?
- Was there anything in the report you disagreed with?
- Was there anything in the report that surprised you?
- If you had to rate how accurate you think the report is in representing you using a scale of 1–5, what score would you give it? A score of 1 is 'completely off the mark' and a score of 5 is 'absolutely represents me'.

> Once you have answered the questions, now complete the following actions:
>
> - Write a paragraph about what completing the task was like for you.
> - What have you learned about yourself by completing this assessment?
> - What impact will knowing your strengths have on you?

Please note: VIA (above) is a free strengths assessment I recommend. I'm also qualified to use a strengths profile assessment with clients that involves a fee and provides you with a debrief so you fully understand the results. Should you wish to know more about that, contact me at carol@strategicachievementcoaching.com.au to arrange a call.

Understanding your strengths is not bragging. This is you being proud of and acknowledging what you are good at. It is not about being arrogant.

SABOTEURS

You must learn how to identify your internal saboteurs, and really understand how they impact you and deter you from hearing your own true voice. Ignoring or discounting them can allow them to take you off course. The negative voices you hear are usually trying to discourage you from doing something by

4: SLAYING THE SABOTEURS

undermining your worth or capacity to act. The powerful saboteur that delayed me from doing my master's degree for twenty years was the voice saying, 'I am not smart enough.'

I was often told as a child, unhelpfully, that I was dumb or stupid, and would never amount to much. This became the internalised message I heard myself say when I felt I was 'not smart enough' for all those years.

Our internal saboteurs may have originated from others' words and actions, but along the way they have become our own. Unfortunately, the negative voices seem to ring louder in our heads than the positive ones, partly because the brain is set to look out for threats and help us avoid them. We often dismiss positive messages as unimportant because our survival mode overrides them.

Simply put, if you want to start something new and succeed, you must defeat your saboteurs.

Several years ago, a friend was undertaking some study with the Positive Intelligence Organisation, led by its founder and primary researcher, Shirzad Charmine. This group's focus was to understand saboteurs, their impact, and how we could combat them to develop our positive-intelligence muscle.

My friend asked me if I would be her guinea pig for an assessment and debrief of the findings. I happily agreed and completed the assessment, and

I was stunned by its accuracy. While I might have given the saboteurs that emerged in the results a different name, the descriptions of them and how they originated were spot on.

First, let me say that everyone's primary saboteur is the Judge. They're like the chairperson of the board and have several co-conspirators or board members. For me, the chief co-conspirators emerged as Stickler (I must get everything exactly right); Hyper-rational (everything must make sense); and Controller (everything must be in order). My initial response to this insight was, 'No wonder I feel so tired.'

This all made so much sense to me, and the insight I gained has since been beneficial to me in many ways.

Things will improve for you, too, if you take time to understand your saboteurs: please don't ignore them. If you get to know your 'enemy within', you can develop efficient tactics to slay them, or at least keep them in their place and prevent them from taking a strong hold on you.

You might be thinking, 'They are so loud, I cannot do anything,' or feeling this book is triggering them even more. If that is the case, do not push yourself too far too fast. Take things slowly. This might be the time to get help from a professional or a trusted friend, and be willing to be vulnerable so change has a chance to happen.

4: SLAYING THE SABOTEURS

The organisation Positive Intelligence exists to 'enable every human to build mental fitness so that they can fulfil their true potential for happiness and contribution'. Their extensive research on people's saboteurs has identified nine prevalent types that people can experience or fall victim to: Judge, Avoider, Controller, Hyper-Achiever, Hyper-Rational, Hyper-Vigilant, Pleaser, Restless, Stickler, and Victim.

EXERCISE 15

REVEALING YOUR SABOTEURS

On the Positive Intelligence website, you will find a convenient assessment tool. The Saboteur Assessment is 'your first step to conquering your Saboteurs – identifying them to expose their lies and limiting beliefs': www.positiveintelligence.com/saboteurs

Once you have taken the saboteurs test, gather your journal and do a reflective exercise. I suggest you complete this within an hour of receiving your report. If you find this challenging, you may want to complete the process with a trusted ally.

Once you've received your report, think about not only the results of the process, but what it was like answering the questions as you completed the assessment. The results are important, but so is your perspective on the identified saboteurs, too. Allow thirty minutes all up – fifteen minutes for the assessment and fifteen minutes for the review. Don't cut yourself short if you need longer.

Here are the questions I'd like you to consider:

- What did you learn about your saboteurs?
- Do you think this is an accurate reflection of your saboteurs?
- What do you think the benefit of knowing your saboteurs will be?

How beneficial did you find this process on a scale of 1–5, where 1 is completely unhelpful and 5 is extremely helpful?

Once you have answered the questions, now complete the following actions:

- Write a paragraph about what completing this task was like for you.
- What have you learned about yourself by completing this assessment?
- What impact will knowing this have on you?

After completing your strengths assessment, reviewing your values and beliefs, and now identifying your saboteurs, you're hopefully getting a sense of your own voice – a product of your thoughts sparking both the helpful voice and the unhelpful voice. You're hearing how you talk about yourself, and learning what matters to you and what might get in your way.

At this point, you might be thinking, 'I sure have some strong saboteurs, now what do I do?'

Stop and think. When you look at the saboteur list, is there one that you think speaks louder than the others, or pops up more frequently? If so, which one would it be? Why do you think this one stands out the most?

Your foundation, made up of values, beliefs, belief systems and strengths, is well-established. You now understand your saboteurs more – they are like the not-so-tasty filling in this sandwich we are building, and you need to learn how to slay them.

Now we're going to look at meaning and purpose in your life.

UNDERSTANDING MEANING AND PURPOSE

Identifying and understanding what has meaning for you and gives you purpose in this stage of your life is a crucial part of hearing your own voice and slaying the saboteurs. To help you determine where you find the inspiration and insight that will encourage you toward the things you are now seeking, we will delve into reflective and spiritual practices that will support you, rather than deter you from your chosen path.

Purpose is about what we aspire to, and meaning relates to how we make sense of the world and our position in it. Your sense of purpose is significant as it guides the decisions you make for your life, and influences behaviour and the goals you set for yourself.

Meaning relates to how you live in a directed and resolute way. This is not about what external influences consider to be right for you. This is what you determine you want and need to do for yourself – what will get you up each morning.

Without purpose or meaning, you risk constant boredom, dissatisfaction, and emptiness. Is this the type of life you want to live? I suspect not.

A friend said to me recently that she didn't think she had a purpose in her life. From my perspective, though, her actions reflect the presence of great intention and principle. She's committed to helping others in whatever way she can, whether that is with emotional or practical support, and that influences everything she does.

You have a purpose, but maybe you have not taken time lately to consider what it is – or maybe you feel you have lost it along the way, as was the case with my friend. It doesn't mean it isn't there. This might be a good time to go investigating and find out exactly what it is, now that you feel you need to review and update your life.

4: SLAYING THE SABOTEURS

Research into purpose and meaning often throws up different points of view, as found by the work of Laura King and Joshua Hicks, published in their 2021 paper, 'The Science of Meaning in Life.' In this article, King and Hicks state that researching meaning and purpose has been sidestepped by many as it has been seen as either too ambiguous or too hard, and that the basis for determining what they are is often based on people's subjective experience rather than something more scientific. While being scientific is important for topics of this nature, one's personal perspective is more important.

A tool that has recently become the main method for identifying purpose and meaning is the Meaning of Life Questionnaire developed by Michael Steger in 2006. You will be referred to this tool in the upcoming exercise.

A definition of meaning derived by summarising a variety of definitions as part of the work of King and colleagues is:

> 'Lives may be experienced as meaningful when they are felt to have significance beyond the trivial or momentary, to have purpose, or to have a coherence that transcends chaos.'

In his work, Steger has gone on to say that meaning is:

> 'the web of connections, understandings, and interpretations that help us comprehend our experiences and formulate plans directing our

energies to the achievement of a desired future. Meaning provides us with the sense that our lives matter, that they make sense, and that they are more than the sum of our seconds, days, and years'.

(King & Hicks, 2021, p.565)

These are quite involved definitions that provide food for thought, and are worth taking the time to consider, without it becoming an overly academic exercise. Suffice to say, meaning and purpose are highly individual things, influenced by philosophical, religious, and societal perspectives, to name a few. There are no right or wrong versions: the judge of yours is you.

One thing that gives me meaning and purpose in life is helping others identify and choose their next direction. This desire to help others influences the decisions I make, how I counteract any discouraging words I might hear, and what I decide to commit my time to. It is one reason I have written this book. I hope to provide a tangible contribution to the body of knowledge that helps others navigate their next path.

Knowing how to determine what gives you meaning and purpose in all stages of your ever-changing life is a multi-purpose tool in your toolkit. It will enable you to make wise decisions and counter the discouraging voices of your saboteurs.

4: SLAYING THE SABOTEURS

Maybe you're wondering, 'Does my purpose have to be big, or can it be small? Can I be happy with being a mother or a thoughtful citizen?' The answer to this is a resounding yes. The perceived size of the purpose is not important. What is important is that it has meaning for you. It will inspire you to press on. It fires you up.

EXERCISE 16

DISCERNING MEANING

Refer to the directions below, and take twenty minutes to complete the Meaning of Life Questionnaire (MLQ) sourced from www.michaelfsteger.com/wp-content/uploads/2012/08/MLQ.pdf

The simple 10-line MLQ will have you answer questions that relate to the presence of meaning in your life, and your search for meaning. The results will provide insight into two things – how present meaning is in your life, and how much time you're investing in searching for it.

Take the first ten minutes of your twenty minutes to complete the questionnaire, and summarise your results by adding up your scores in the two categories of 'presence' and 'search' – the directions sit below the ten rating lines.

> Then take the remaining ten minutes to reflect on the result. Which has the highest score? Is the presence of meaning the higher factor, or is searching for meaning the highest factor? What do you think might be the reason for this?
>
> Refer to this document for more information about what the questionnaire measures:
>
> www.michaelfsteger.com/wp-content/uploads/2013/12/MLQ-description-scoring-and-feedback-packet.pdf

Does this activity prompt you to do something different? If so, document the steps you want to take in your journal because of completing this questionnaire. Ideally, it will have provided some insights about where to focus your energies to orient you in the direction you wish to take along your next path.

You might think, 'I really do not know how to answer these questions.' Try not to overthink your answers. Remember, if this is a starting point for you, then giving this a try will provide you with understanding. Even a beginner's understanding is helpful, and now you will have something to build on.

4: SLAYING THE SABOTEURS

DESCRIBING YOURSELF

In Chapter 1, you told your story. We are now looking at how you describe the main character in your story – you. This section looks at how you honour yourself, and examines where you place yourself in your pursuits and relationships, as this affects how you value what you want and need. This is about the placement of you in your story, in what you do, and how you do it.

Findings emanating from my doctoral thesis in 2021 resulted in what I call, 'Formulation of self', five self-related attitudes that influence our perspective of self, what we do, and how we interrelate.

FORMULATION OF SELF-RELATED ATTITUDES

The list below outlines the five types of attitudes we have about ourselves:

1. Self-efficacy: Relates to the belief that we have the ability and competencies to achieve a desired outcome. This can vary over time, as I know it has for me. When I was younger, I had a much lower belief in my capabilities. Now, with experience and a willingness and desire to continue to grow, my level of self-efficacy has increased.
2. Self-belief: Relates to our confidence in our ability and judgement. Because of some

experiences I have outlined so far in this book, you may have concluded that my self-belief was lower when I was younger, and that is true. In the intervening period since I lost my husband, where I have had to face and overcome many challenges, my self-belief and self-efficacy have both grown.

3. Self-esteem (global): This is our overall assessment of our worth. We distinguish this as global because individuals can have different levels of self-esteem. For example, I have high self-esteem in my ability to coach, but my self-esteem is a lot lower when it relates to my ability to do public speaking. However, my global self-esteem is high because I know I am a competent person overall, but I possess different competencies depending on what I want or need to do.

4. Self-perception: This aspect considers how I see myself. This aligns with how I would describe myself to someone else: I would say I am a caring person who loves people and wants to make a difference by helping them live their best life.

5. Self-conception: This is different from self-perception as it considers how others see us. While we have our own view of ourselves, others shape how we form that view and ultimately arrive at our self-conception. I know others see me as strong, forthright, capable, and non-nonsense. It appears that

4: SLAYING THE SABOTEURS

people can pick up these aspects about me quickly in the way I present myself.

The above self-related attitudes all play important roles in forming the voice we hear within. Ignore it at your peril – and understand the risks if you do. Ignoring your voice will limit your capacity to slay your saboteurs.

Your attitudes and what you project about yourself will affect how others relate to you. You set the tone, and they will follow. In my thirties, I didn't see myself as a strong character, and would always place myself as the weaker person in a conversation or a relationship, or an interaction. I would always see myself as second best, and not as good as the other party. That was my voice: 'I don't measure up to them.' That was a limiting belief, and it wasn't helpful.

Through a lot of internal work, as well as support and encouragement from others over time, I learned how to better honour myself, and not at anyone else's expense. When I changed how I felt about myself and how I showed up, others' responses changed as well. How I chose to be present, what I heard, and how I described and talked about myself made a difference.

You may think, 'Taking time to think about how I describe myself seems strange to me.' If you are feeling unsettled in your life, your choice is simple: either work for underlying fulfilment or end up with debilitating discontent. Choosing the former as your goal will contribute to becoming more comfortable in your own skin.

When I finally heard what my voice was actually saying in my own story, and changed the recording, I felt so much more pride in myself, and I also felt much more comfortable with who I am. It wasn't a struggle every day to just be me.

I hope it will be the same for you, and this process will make it easier to just be yourself.

EXERCISE 17

UNDERSTANDING YOUR SELF-RELATED ATTITUDES

Return to your journal in your chosen location and allow yourself up to thirty minutes to do this task. Remember, it's important to undertake tasks such as this without interruptions.

Step 1

Use the Scale column in the worksheet below to rate how you see your competency related to each attitude, using a scale of 1–10, where 1 is low, 5 is moderate, and 10 is high. For example, 'My self-esteem is low so I will scale that a 3.'

4: SLAYING THE SABOTEURS

Remember, try not to overthink it. Trust your instincts. It's likely that the first number you think of will be the most accurate.

Attitude Ratings Worksheet

ATTITUDE	SCALE (1-10)	RATING (PRIORITY)	COMMENT
Self-efficacy			
Self-belief			
Self-esteem (global)			
Self-perception			
Self-conception			

Step 2

In the Rating column, on a scale of 1–5 rate how important you think each of the attitudes is in your life. For example, 'Even though I scaled myself as a 3 in self-belief, I feel it is the most important attitude for my success, so I rate it as 5. I rate self-efficacy as 4, self-esteem as 3, self-perception as 2, and self-conception as 1, the least important to me in the context of this exercise.'

This will help you see the importance you place on each attitude and how this might impact how you see yourself and what you might choose to do next. Consider the one you rate the highest. How does that influence how you see yourself? Is it supportive? Is it helpful to you when slaying the saboteurs? If so, how? If not, why not? What does seeing these items rated in this way do for your self-image? What might you do differently as a result?

You might struggle with this and say, 'I do not know how to rate myself on these items.' If it's easier, start with rating someone you admire and respect so that you familiarise yourself with a rating scale. By doing that for someone else first, you will gain a level of familiarity.

CONCLUSION

This chapter has covered a lot of territory. It's explored values, beliefs, and strengths; saboteurs and their impact; purpose and meaning; and how you define yourself.

By placing these things centre stage, you are better positioned to drown out the external noise and internal saboteurs that might interfere with you hearing what you want. Take your values, purpose, and strengths more seriously. Learn to treat them

4: SLAYING THE SABOTEURS

with respect – your own voice is your most trusted ally as you journey on.

Now you have done all the background work in preparation for your new journey. It's time to pack your bag and get ready to go. The next chapter will explore the equipment and supplies you need to travel with ease and reach your destination. You don't need to overpack. There is a weight limit for this trip. The key is not to carry excess baggage as you journey along your next path.

5

PACK YOUR BAG

You cannot climb a peak or walk the Camino trail unless you have packed the right gear, because you are aiming for more than survival: accomplishment is your goal. So, let's determine what you need in your bag as you set forth.

All journeys occur in stages over time, and you need to assemble a toolkit of skills, beliefs, attitudes, and aptitudes to prepare yourself before you take off. This isn't about your value as a person; this is about your capacity and the provisions you will need with you to sustain you along the way.

When I was learning to fly solo through life after becoming a widow, I felt scared and constantly out of my depth. Realising I could not continue that way, I needed to revise and repack the contents in my bag, otherwise I would not survive the trip. I needed to remove all self-doubt and add self-advocacy to my kit bag.

Many people love going to Bunnings (a major hardware store in Australia), but I had only been there with an expert, my husband. When I went alone for the first time after my husband died, I stood in the vast space, frozen and terrified. I realised later that I had expected to be able to go in, find the one thing I wanted, and walk out after paying, without browsing or asking for help, or feeling any emotion about doing this alone for the first time. Wrong.

After that experience, my resolution was that each day I would try to use something from my toolkit to sustain me. The next time I went, I asked for what I needed, even though the assistant was unhelpful and condescending. I stuck to my guns despite him, and got what I wanted.

Even though my clients' issues are all unique, the journey through change is the same; however, what they might pack in their bags differs from person to person. Most importantly, everyone needs to pack the right items. Remember, though, the particular items you need can also change from time to time along the way.

Let's now delve into several essential skills that will equip you to travel your next path successfully. While these ideas are being teased out separately and sequentially here, you might need to think about how they work together, and develop them concurrently.

First, self-agency and self-advocacy explore how you ask for what you need. You'll learn to hear your own voice, putting you in a position to use it to your advantage.

Then we will consider positive goal setting using my SIMPLE Goals framework. This approach looks at how you articulate your goals so they align with your values and beliefs, and are supportive of what gives you meaning and purpose in your life.

Next, we consider intent, intentions, and intentionality, followed by methods you can use to add spiritual practices to help you maintain your wellbeing along the way. The chapter concludes by reviewing resources such as friends and supportive habits – financial and relational – at your disposal to sustain you as you navigate your next path.

LEARN TO SPEAK UP FOR YOURSELF

Together, self-agency and self-advocacy provide you with the ability to better hear your own voice, and honour yourself and what you need – but how do they differ?

Self-agency is the sense of control you feel in your life, and the opposite of apathy, inertia, and idleness. Without self-agency, you won't be in a good position to travel your next path and bring about the changes you seek, whatever you choose them to be. When you have self-agency, you take confident action and exercise sound judgement. When you do not exercise your self-agency, you become stuck and indecisive, rely on poor judgement, and take fearful action – including taking no action at all.

When learning to master self-agency, there are several strategies you can apply. In all situations, remember to stay as calm as you can. Source quality information, whether you are keeping up with world events, learning something new, or weighing up a decision about your life. Be willing to challenge your assumptions. Actively manage your emotions so they are supportive of you. Exercise your critical-thinking skills so you make well-reasoned decisions.

Self-advocacy is exercising your agency to do what you want and need to do in order to make changes in your life. There are three key parts to self-advocacy: exploration, communication, and action:

1. Exploration involves learning what you need in order to participate in decisions and determine your own life, identifying your rights and responsibilities, and learning how to get quality information.
2. Communication, as part of self-advocacy, is speaking up for yourself, and seeking others who will support you when you need help.
3. Action involves developing strategies, problem-solving, and doing what you need to do to take you in the direction you wish to go.

Self-agency and self-advocacy go hand in hand. Knowing you can act is not enough. You must do the exploration and the actions – and, when necessary, communicate them. This is you setting limits on what you will accept and do for yourself, and communicating that to others when necessary. Without self-agency and self-advocacy, you are likely to stagnate, and experience increasing levels of discontent and frustration.

When you develop these tools, you'll be well equipped to use them when you face a roadblock or challenge. I cannot tell you how important these skills have been for me since becoming a widow and needing to discern and travel a completely different path in life.

The workplace is one arena where our self-agency and self-advocacy skills can be tested from time to time. I was once verbally attacked by a senior colleague in a public place and felt quite intimidated. No words came out of my mouth as I struggled to speak. Realising I was undeserving of this treatment, I politely indicated I needed to leave. I knew because of self-agency that I didn't have to put up with this treatment, so I advocated for myself and walked away.

When you discover, explore, and apply self-agency and self-advocacy, they both help you to better hear your own voice, honour yourself and what you need, and do what you want to do.

In most situations, we have a choice, so what choice do you make? Do you advocate on your own behalf or stay silent?

You might ask, 'How will I know when I need to use self-agency and self-advocacy? I don't know what I'm missing.' You will know if you are in a situation that feels scary, uneasy, or intimidating. Start small and find a safe environment with someone you trust to practise developing your skills in this area.

EXERCISE 18

TASK ASSESSMENT

For the purposes of this exercise, I will share a personal experience that demonstrates how I called on skills of self-advocacy and self-agency.

One task I was avoiding after losing my husband was sorting through the tools that had meant so much to him. Disposing of them felt like I was throwing him away. There were a number of things holding me back, some emotional and others more practical.

After many attempts with no successful outcome, I finally found someone who could help me with this task, and I could sort through his tools in a way that respected him and the items involved. My local Men's Shed (an Australia-wide men's support group) provided the necessary assistance at a time when I was better equipped emotionally to deal with this hard task.

5: PACK YOUR BAG

The tools that were of value were distributed to groups who could benefit from them. Metal and other items that could be recycled were given to relevant parties. What was of no value was taken to a disposal centre, or I disposed of them over time.

I found a new sense of freedom from doing such a difficult task while being respectful to myself and my late husband.

Using insights gained from reading about my experience, now think about your own situation. Find your favourite location where you won't be interrupted and take fifteen minutes to follow these four steps:

1. Begin by thinking about tasks or situations you like to avoid. Identifying these will help you realise where you need more agency. For example, it was going to Bunnings for me. For you, it might be speaking up in a meeting.
2. Write out what makes you want to avoid the task or situation. If you don't like to speak up in meetings, what is it you dislike about that?
3. Think about how applying the tools of self-advocacy, such as communication, exploration and action, could help you become better equipped to face a situation you prefer to avoid, like being more willing to speak up in a meeting.

4. Once you have thought about this, think about what would be different for you if you could face this task or situation by using your self-agency and self-advocacy. Whatever comes up for you are things you can add into your toolkit if you are willing to spend time developing them.

Remember, if this gets a bit too scary for you, take a break. Come back to it when you feel ready to consider it in more depth. Do not rush yourself through this. Maybe you're not sure where to start. Which do you feel is easier to understand? Self-agency or self-advocacy? Start with that one.

SIMPLE GOAL SETTING

The most referenced framework for setting measurable goals, first outlined in 1981 by George T Doran, is SMART goals – Specific, Measurable, Achievable, Realistic or Relevant, and Time-bound. However, I found that model was not enough for me, so I developed the SIMPLE approach to goal setting, outlined next.

5: PACK YOUR BAG

SIMPLE Goal-Setting Approach

S	SAFE	This relates to the fact that the goals you set for yourself are both psychologically and physically safe. Of course, you want to set goals that stretch you, but not ones that will create (debilitating) fear or put you at risk. Example: I will complete my newly revised job application by the end of the week. (There might be some challenges in doing this, but it is doable.)
I	INDIVIDUAL INTEGRATED INTENTIONAL	Individual – The goal is unique to you. Integrated – The goal fits with your overall lifestyle desires Intentional – There is a reason and purpose behind why this goal has been set. It fits with your desired strategic intent. It fits with the values and vision you have for yourself. Example: I am going to help at the Hope charity as I want to make a difference to children who are doing it tough and having a hard start in life.
M	MEANINGFUL	This relates to the fact that the goal(s) you set have meaning for you. Ideally, they relate to your strengths and values and how you want to contribute to the world you are in. Example: I am going to volunteer at the homeless shelter once a week for the next three months so I can give something to those in need. (Your goal could be your desire to give back and you value community.)

P	PERSONAL	This means there is no external factor making you set a specific goal. It is your personal choice to act on the stated goal.
		Example: Working at the homeless shelter is a personal choice. There is no mandated reason to do this.
L	LEGITIMATE	Whatever goal you set must be within your power to achieve.
		Example: You're not going to fly a plane tomorrow when you have never had a flying lesson. However, if you are a pilot, you may be desiring to go a new route, or fly a different type of plane.
E	ENERGISING, EMPOWERING, ENGAGING	This relates to the fact that the goals you set encourage or drive you to act. They help you to move towards (approach) something that has meaning for you.
		Example: The thought of helping the homeless brings you joy, and you get excited and energised by the prospect. It is a joy, not a chore.

When I used this approach, I found that my goals connected to my heart, not just my head, so I now set SIMPLE SMART goals. You can readily find information about SMART goals in books and online, if this is a new concept for you. If you need to find out more, I remind you that it stands for:

- **S**pecific
- **M**easurable
- **A**chievable

5: PACK YOUR BAG

- **R**ealistic or **R**elevant
- **T**ime-bound or **T**imely

Here, I want to focus on SIMPLE goals, their intent, and what they can do to help you along your next path.

The objective is that you make choices and create goals that take you towards what you seek, inspire you to keep going, and help you last the distance. There is more to goal setting than just being SMART. The primary aim of SMART goals is to ensure accountability and movement. The SIMPLE goal framework considers goals that have meaning for you.

All of your considerations in previous chapters can now come together to help inform the goals you want to set for yourself to enhance your likelihood of navigating your next path successfully.

SIMPLE goals will not only help you envision your future, but they will also help you stay connected and move towards your desired future because they are not just tasks. The SIMPLE approach ensures you set goals that matter, and this enables you to maintain focus – not just because you want to set a deadline, which is important, but because achieving the goal gives you something you desire that is important for you. Therefore, the E in SIMPLE is especially important – 'energising', 'empowering' and 'engaging': you will want to work on goals that will make your life richer. However, to reach the E, the other steps in SIMPLE must be considered.

They all work together to help with the development of meaningful goals.

Your head will only get you so far, but following your heart is likely to take you further. SMART goals emanate from your thoughts. SIMPLE goals emanate from your heart.

Back in 2021, I retired my old business and started a new one. In doing this, I realised I was going to need a website and had no idea how to do this for myself. I needed to find an approach that I knew I would be able to navigate, even though there were likely to be moments I found challenging. I found a small-business owner who I thought could give me what I needed in a manageable timeframe. I found her approach to be warm and comforting, even 'safe' (S).

The development of this website was also 'integrated' (I) because it was part of my goal of establishing my new business. The direction this new business was taking was 'meaningful' (M) for me because I had homed in more precisely on my target client base. The website developer and I had an initial discussion to understand what was involved and what I would need – and determined that it would be possible to have my website up and running within three months.

Setting up this website was not something anyone had forced me to do, so that made it 'personal' (P). It was 'legitimate' (L) and within my abilities

5: PACK YOUR BAG

in the sense that I could afford to pay someone to do it, and I could also provide the relevant input for the development of the site. I also had friends who could help me put together the information I needed. When I found there were aspects I couldn't do myself, I employed different people with the skills to provide what I needed, which was the copy to go on the website. When I saw the result, I was so proud of the website, and how it represented my business in such a professional way. This made it energising, empowering, and engaging (E).

When you set goals using the SIMPLE framework, you can exploit your brain's ability to create something positive, an important part of enhancing your wellbeing. You might dispute this by saying, 'I'm used to setting SMART goals. Can't I just use that model? Why make it more complicated?' Yes, you can use it, but it will only get you some of the way. If you combine the steps in SIMPLE and SMART, you'll stick to your path longer and go further, taking you closer to reaching your desired destination.

EXERCISE 19

SIMPLE SMART GOAL DEVELOPMENT

Next, you will find a worksheet you can use to develop SIMPLE goals that, once created, can then be crafted into a SIMPLE SMART goal format. Before completing your worksheet, I have provided a worked example to illustrate how to undertake the process of writing your SIMPLE SMART goal.

Simple Smart Goal Development Worksheet

DRAFT GOAL	
This space is provided for you to write your draft goal.	
To start my own community organic gardening business in rural Victoria (Australia) so I can leave my current corporate role and suburban life and live a life that is purposeful and considerate, and positively nurtures my wellbeing.	
SIMPLE GOAL FRAMEWORK	
SAFE	*Review your draft goal and outline why and how it meets the Safe aspect.* It requires a stretch but not one that is beyond my capabilities. It will have positive emotional and physical benefits.

INDIVIDUAL, INTEGRATED, AND INTENTIONAL	*Review your draft goal and outline why and how it meets the Individual, Integrated and Intentional aspect.*
	Individual – I can achieve much of this goal on my own – and seek help as needed
	Integrated – fits with my overall lifestyle intent
	Intentional – it is based on a deliberate choice for the particular lifestyle I crave
MEANINGFUL	*Review your draft goal and outline why and how it meets the Meaningful aspect.*
	This has meaning because it sets me up to live a life that is congruent with my personal desires, needs and what I feel is important.
PERSONAL	*Review your draft goal and outline why and how it meets the Personal aspect.*
	There is no coercion. This is the lifestyle I choose after long consideration.
LEGITIMATE	*Review your draft and outline why and how it meets the Legitimate aspect.*
	I have the right training and some experience, and I can establish suitable connections and collaborations, giving me a high likelihood of success.

ENERGISING, EMPOWERING, AND ENGAGING	*Review your draft goal and outline why and how it meets the Energising, Empowering and Engaging aspect.* There is strong alignment with what I stand for personally, socially, and environmentally. There is great energy in being able to legitimately and meaningfully engage with nature and see it grow, and experience the joy I can provide to others by offering the wider community the chance to join in.
SIMPLE SMART GOAL *After using this SIMPLE framework, reword your goal so it also fits with the SMART goal framework, to align with both your heart and your head.* Find and acquire a suitable location for the garden and for living in by the end of 2026 (twelve months). Set up initial collaborations by September 2026 (nine months) in preparation. Have the first participants join the garden by June 2027 (eighteen months).	

Give yourself an hour in a pleasant space where you will be uninterrupted, as you will need to tune into your own voice. You might need a break while completing this goal, so work for twenty-five minutes, have a five-minute rest, then come back to it for the remaining time. Have a copy of the explanation of SIMPLE goals next to you to help you as you work through the worksheet.

You might think, 'This framework doesn't seem SIMPLE to me.' If that's the case, you don't have to start with the S if that doesn't work for you. Pick one of the other aspects – the I, the M, the P, the L, or the E – and start there. You don't have to start at the top and work down. It's arranged this way so it is easy to remember the approach, but it's not meant to imply a linear approach when working through it.

DRAFT GOAL	
This space is provided for you to write your draft goal.	
SIMPLE GOAL FRAMEWORK	
Safe	Review your draft goal and outline why and how it meets the Safe aspect.
Individual, Integrated, and Intentional	Review your draft goal and outline why and how it meets the Individual, Integrated and Intentional aspect.
Meaningful	Review your draft goal and outline why and how it meets the Meaningful aspect.
Personal	Review your draft goal and outline why and how it meets the Personal aspect.
Legitimate	This means you have the skills and abilities needed to do what you want and need to do.
Energising, Empowering, and Engaging	Review your draft goal and outline why and how it meets the Energising, Empowering and Engaging aspect.

> **SIMPLE SMART GOAL**
> After using this SIMPLE framework, reword your goal so it also fits with the SMART goal framework, to align with both your heart and your head.

This activity may require you to work at it on numerous occasions until you get it to a point you are happy with and that sits comfortably with both your head and heart. Do not try to rush this process, as it will be one of the critical steps helping you to successfully step out on your next path.

If you have more than one goal you are working towards, you might need to do this process more than once. If you have multiple goals, the *integrated* aspect of the framework is vitally important as you do not want your goals conflicting with each other and making your path more difficult.

THE SECRET TO CHANGING HABITS

This section is about intent, intention, and being intentional, and even though these words sound very similar, they're quite different.

Intent: The focus of your attention, your motive, or your purpose. You have a firm resolve to get it done. What destination point are you focusing on – your end goal or a point along the way? Using my Bunnings experience as a simple example, my intent was to get what I needed from the hardware store and leave.

5: PACK YOUR BAG

Intention: The act of determining the steps you will take to achieve a result or reach a destination point. My intention was to drive to Bunnings to find and purchase the item I needed. Intentions can be small; they do not have to be large in their impact. One intention may be as simple as wanting to be less critical.

Intentional: Being willing to do what is important, even if it is difficult. Even though I was terrified of going to Bunnings for the first time on my own, I faced the situation rather than avoiding it, having previously decided I would not make decisions from a position of fear. Being intentional is about being clear on exactly what you want to focus your energies and efforts on. This is about developing helpful habits that produce desired outcomes, moving them from a wish to a want. Your intent, your intentions, and being intentional all help you shift goals from something you wish for to something you get.

Employing the tools of intent, intentions and being intentional means establishing helpful mechanisms that will enable you to change your old habits and form new habits that specifically prepare you to navigate your next path.

When I became a postgraduate lecturer in coaching and leadership with the Australian Institute of Professional Counsellors (AIPC) Professional Courses in February 2023, my intent was to help coaches become informed in how they practise, rather than being mechanical in their approach. I had not lectured for at least eight years, and some units I was teaching were completely new to me. My intention was to provide students with the best available information on the subject areas we covered, and give them the opportunity to ask questions to help expand their understanding. Being intentional meant creating a learning experience that went beyond simply conveying information to them. I was intentional in ensuring I used all the knowledge available, which included that possessed by my students, as well as my own knowledge and understanding.

I stepped up and faced the challenge. With a willingness to learn, I ensured that my students and I all had a richer encounter, making the learning process more fruitful for everyone involved. I doubt this would have happened to the extent it did without employing my intent, defining my intention, and being intentional.

By applying intent and intention, and being intentional, you too will be able to adopt new habits that will enable you to successfully navigate your next path. If you are not convinced, think about a time you achieved something you set out to do. What do you think your intent was at that time? How can you act now with more intent?

EXERCISE 20

BECOME INTENTIONAL

Use your journal in your preferred location and allow yourself fifteen minutes. Remember, starting small is okay. Think about a habit you might like to change, e.g. biting your nails, or watching a lot of TV. Answer the following questions about that habit:

- Why do you want to stop that habit? This is your intent.
- What steps will you take to stop the habit? What are your intentions?
- What will be the first step you take (reward or outcome) when you stop your habit? That's being intentional.

You might struggle with this or think it seems insignificant. The choice you have is to be mindful about what you do, or mindless and just float along. You decide.

FROM TO-DO TO TA-DA

You cannot overestimate the importance of giving to yourself. This is how you keep yourself charged and able to deal with challenges, doubts, or delays along your next path. This is about self-care and accepting that this needs to be a priority for you.

Self-care includes the deliberate actions you take to support your own wellbeing. They can be small, like buying yourself a nice cup of tea in a tranquil location after a busy day, or extensive, like going away for a few days with a close friend for peace, quiet, and trusted companionship. Anything that nurtures you is self-care – and requires you to notice what you are observing about yourself and what is affecting you, then do something about it.

Self-care is not about being selfish, and never occurs at the expense of someone else. It can come in many forms:

- Physical self-care: Taking care of your body so that it runs efficiently.
    - I began regular hydrotherapy initially to recover from hip-replacement surgery, then on an ongoing basis to provide me with deliberate times to exercise and move my body.
- Social self-care: Mixing with others such as friends and family, and people who nurture you and help you grow and

5: PACK YOUR BAG

develop. This is an important form of self-care that can often be overlooked.
- I make sure I catch up with friends at least once a week. This is a priority for me, especially now I live alone.

- Mental self-care: What we fill our minds with. Is it helpful input or unhelpful?
    - I have exercised mental self-care by choosing to no longer watch the news, as it was only causing me to feel sadder, and that was not helping me.

- Spiritual self-care: Activities that help you develop a deeper sense of meaning. This can include such things as mindfulness, spending time in nature, meditation, or prayer. It can involve religious practices if that is important for you.
    - Walking by the river each day, meditating, and practising mindfulness are all ways I seek to nurture my spirit.

- Emotional self-care: Having strategies you can call on when you experience negative emotions, for example, anger, sadness, or feeling anxious. This might involve you talking to a trusted friend or family member, seeking professional help, or doing something you consider fun.
    - When I'm feeling emotionally challenged, I ring a friend and we chat it out. I think having a

'recreational whinge' is helpful to distil the unhelpful emotions. You can express your discomfort or challenge with a trusted party, not because you need them to do anything, but because it is a chance for you to dilute the intensity of what you are feeling in a safe and helpful way. Leverage the saying, 'A problem shared is a problem halved.'

It's always important to prioritise self-care, but there might be times when you need more than a simple indulgence. It may mean an entire program of support if the need arises, or it can simply be a series of one-off events. Do not ignore the need for self-care, otherwise you will reach the limit of what you can handle, and risk becoming completely derailed or needing a long time to get yourself back on track.

Self-care is not a luxury item. It is an essential part of your toolkit, and you need to make room for it in your travel bag so it can sustain you the entire distance. Without it, you risk giving up.

The self-care strategy you choose to use at any one time will depend on what you are facing then, so create your own effective self-care plan, and tailor it to your specific needs and lifestyle. This is your best preventative medicine, helping you to avoid becoming overwhelmed or overstressed, which would make it difficult for you to achieve your next important goals.

5: PACK YOUR BAG

What you need may also change over time as you become more aware of what you find most helpful. I recently introduced meditation alongside mindfulness to help me get through a particularly challenging time that I faced as I wrote this book, which already required a lot from me.

Ignoring self-care for too long can lead to burnout, which can be difficult to recover from. If you feel you are at a point of burnout, it is best to seek help to support you so you feel equipped to take action, rather than stumble on alone.

When my husband died, my circumstances changed dramatically, and I couldn't overlook or ignore the challenge of learning to live alone. Doing what I had done before would not have gotten me through. Experiencing compound and complex grief took up a lot of my energy, and my emotional bandwidth was at an all-time low. I could not continue the way I was. It was not an option. Therefore, I incorporated more nurturing self-care activities into my daily life.

I started routinely going down by the river, allowing me to sit, enjoy nature, and take time out from what I was feeling. I spent more time with those who cared about me so I felt loved and cared for. I began mindfulness practices that allowed me to clear away all the voices and noise in my head telling me what I could or could no longer do now I was on my own.

Those self-care activities gave me a tonic to help me through each day, as that was a difficult time in my life. Each time I did one of those self-nurturing acts, I could feel the tension in my body ease, helping me ensure my body was not consistently under stress, and allowing for restoration.

Many years on from the loss of my husband, I still do these things as I need them, and they keep me functional, and help me remain charged and able to face challenges and obstacles as they occur. They can do the same for you.

You might think, 'I can't do self-care all the time. Is it okay not to?' If doing a self-care activity feels like it's a burden rather than a benefit, don't do it. They should always be helpful.

EXERCISE 21

DEVELOPING A TA-DA LIST

Now, we're going to create a ta-da list. This is a list of what you've achieved, as opposed to a to-do list of what you have yet to do. For the next seven days, take ten minutes at the end of each day and write your ta-da list of the things you've done that day.

If you get three things done in a day, give yourself a clap. Should you get five things done in a day, shout yourself a small treat, like a nice cup of tea in a favourite spot. If you get seven things done in a day, watch an episode of your favourite show. However, should you be able to get ten things done in a day, go out and celebrate.

Each of these actions is an example of self-care based on the significance or extent of what you're celebrating. You might think, 'But what if I forget to do it after a busy day?' One way to get around that could be to set a reminder on your phone for, say, 4:45 pm, so it reminds you that this is your ta-da list time. Be intentional and don't leave the office until it's done.

SPIRITUAL SELF-CARE AND WHY IT MATTERS

Spiritual self-care relates to the framework, principles, morals, and rituals that provide you with meaning in your life, and help you maintain focus, especially when the going gets tough. While these elements are part of self-care, it is important not to draw on them solely when you feel you are in trouble. Spiritual practices can guide you as you navigate your way in the world on a day-to-day basis. You might need to dial them up or down as required, but it helps you if they are a natural part of your daily routine.

Find ways that mean something to you: connecting with nature, meditation, reading something inspirational, reflecting through a journal, connecting with others, or simply practising gratitude. If they are part of your worldview, you will also include religious practices.

One of the spiritual practices I choose is prayer. I find it nurturing to hand over my struggles to someone I perceive as greater than myself. It helps me feel like I am sharing my load, making it lighter for me to carry.

Spiritual self-care does not relate solely to religious practices, but it can include them. Activities like being in nature are not specifically part of any formalised religious practice. These practices typically provide a path to personal growth, and connection to the larger community. They also affect the relationships you form and the meaning you place on them.

I've joined several communities of practice centred on topics I'm interested in so I can engage with people from more diverse backgrounds than my own, expanding how I see and connect to the world. While there is a cognitive benefit to these activities, I also nurture my spirit as it becomes more malleable and open to new experiences that help me grow as an individual.

Understanding spirituality will help you thrive and achieve the deep fulfilment you are seeking as you travel along your next path. I don't know about you, but the more I nurture my spirit, the more a-ha moments I seem to have. My spiritual practices have

5: PACK YOUR BAG

me better placed to experience awe, providing me with a greater sense of wonder and appreciation for what is taking place around me.

I was struggling to cope with life after losing a friend because of cancer very suddenly in the second half of 2023. All the things I knew how to do were not enough. Developing a skin condition because of stress didn't help me, so I decided to extend my spiritual practices to include devoted time for mindfulness. That was like giving my mind time to have a restoring power nap, so I had more energy and space for what came next. It helped me to eliminate confusion and facilitate clarity of mind. With this, I was better placed to make wiser decisions and concentrate more fully on tasks I needed to complete. Doing this nurtured my mind and my spirit, and reduced my sense of overwhelm and incapacitation.

When the going gets tough, the tough get going – and spiritual practices help you to be tough enough to face life's challenges and come out victorious. You might think you are not a religious person, but you don't have to be religious to be spiritual. It's simply about developing a new level of conscious awareness of what is going on around you, instead of walking around in a daze.

EXERCISE 22

HOW YOU NURTURE YOUR SPIRITUAL WELLBEING

Find a welcoming place where you'll be able to sit, reflect, and simply observe what is around you. It might be near water, or have a good view, or interesting artwork, or be in a favourite room. Take fifteen minutes in your pleasant space and think about five things you do regularly to nurture yourself that connect you to your world and your place in it, such as writing a gratitude journal, general journaling, walking the dog in the evening to wind down at the end of the day, meditating or praying. Once you have listed the five things, rank them in the order you find the most nurturing.

Each of these activities are ways you can nurture your spiritual wellbeing and positively contribute to your overall sense of wellbeing.

5: PACK YOUR BAG

> Often, we do things on autopilot or mindlessly, and do not take time to consider their value to us. This activity can help you to either establish a routine for deliberate spiritual practices, or refine the one you already have. You will then have your collection of spiritual practices mapped out to help orient you in your desired direction and keep you healthy so you can travel your next path successfully.

Even though you may be thinking you're not really a spiritual person, we all have a spiritual side to us. Take the time to consider this by doing the exercise above. What you find about yourself may pleasantly surprise you.

REVIEW YOUR TRAVEL BAG

Now it's time to undertake a review of the resources you have, and those you might need to help you walk this new path. We've just talked here about your internal resources to put in your toolkit. Now we're going to look at some external resources you need to help get you through – the supplies you might need to draw into your kit bag rather than draw from it.

Having worked through the exercises in this book to this point, you will have a clear idea of what matters to you, and this knowledge will help you determine what else you might need to help you traverse the path ahead. Some examples might be inspirational books or quotes, a support crew, professional help, training, technology, financial resources, and medical resources.

If you have decided you want to change careers, for example, will you need to undertake further study? Find out. Then, determine what financial reserves you will need to enable you to do that. Will you need to pay for the education up front, or can you pay later? The answer will determine what you need to do in preparation.

Knowing the gaps between where you are now and where you want to be will help you decipher what else needs to go into that kit bag.

If you feel you can't do this alone, you will need external support to get you through it, like I did. When I was setting up my business website, my various fears of technology were rearing their ugly heads. However, it was too late to turn back, so I had to find a way to keep going. I sought help from my support crew – my inner circle of friends – and used my financial resources to get extra help to assist me in overcoming my blockages. My kit bag then included my support crew, financial resources, and external help.

You do not want to be under-resourced or run out of what you need as you are making your way on your new path, with no way of getting what you need. If you feel you don't have external resources to draw on, start with a trusted friend.

5: PACK YOUR BAG

EXERCISE 23

RESOURCE INVENTORY

Take out your journal in your favourite location again. Allow fifteen minutes to write an inventory of external resources you can draw on – friends, finances, organisations you belong to, education resources, technical skills, etc.

After writing your inventory, pick two things that would help you achieve your SIMPLE goal. If you come up with more than two, so be it, but you might start to feel overwhelmed. You don't want to over-pack your kit bag, so let's not have excess baggage either. This is about ensuring you have enough of the things you need, without being overloaded.

If you feel you need too many things and don't know where or how to get them, begin with a list of what you need. Then mark each item according to whether you think they'll be easy or hard to get. Determine when you might need them. Then pick one simple thing to get now, and start there.

Work through your list, gathering what you need by alternating between an easy item and a more difficult one, as you progress through your journey. Don't just face all the hard stuff at once.

CONCLUSION

In this chapter, we've considered the equipment you'll need to have access to for success. We reviewed internal factors such as self-advocacy and self-agency; goals; intent, intentions and being intentional; giving to self; and spiritual practices.

While these things are vital, there are also external factors that ensure you are well-equipped for your journey. These include such things as technology, finance, books, medicine, a support crew, and professional help. Stop thinking you can embark on your travels without an updated toolkit, and begin ensuring you have all the tools you need.

When you have packed your bag, you are ready to go. In the next chapter, you will find out how to recognise that you have arrived, and that you are in good shape.

6

SUCCESS – WHAT DOES IT LOOK LIKE?

As you navigate any new path, strategically placed checkpoints will tell you that you are heading in the right direction. To determine what those checkpoints are for you, you need to define what success will look like, and know how to measure your progress.

The checkpoints are not there to restrict you and make everything difficult. They are the equivalent to welcome rest stops when you go on a long trip, where you 'stop, revive, survive' (a road-safety campaign slogan in my home state). They give you a chance to happily celebrate all your achievements along the way, and help you stay focused on the goals and objectives you've set for yourself.

> 'If you don't define your own personal views about what you want from life and how you want to live it, chances are you will never be able to live a satisfied life.'

Elena Agaragimova, organisational development specialist and author of Shift, wrote the above words in a LinkedIn post on 3 October 2018 entitled, 'Defining your own Success.'

Determining and reviewing what success looks like begins with developing success criteria. Once you determine those, you can measure success meaningfully. What reflective practices will support you or support this process? Review how you keep the intent and intentions you outlined in Chapter 5 uppermost in your mind. Identify and establish ways to keep yourself accountable and on track.

SUCCESS CRITERIA

Success criteria describe markers you select to show you've succeeded in a way that you find meaningful and sustaining. This is not about establishing rigid rules. It's about setting up encouragers that allow you to celebrate success.

Success criteria will include small things like booking into a course that you've always wanted to do, or growing your friendship group, or reaching a savings target. They can be objectives on their own, or steps towards a bigger goal, like making a particular phone call on a given day instead of putting it off again, even though you know it will take you one step closer to what you want.

6: SUCCESS – WHAT DOES IT LOOK LIKE?

Your personally customised success criteria also ensure you follow your own life plans, rather than being influenced to take a detour and end up somewhere you don't want to be. With stated criteria, your version of success becomes doable.

I once had to apply for a new role in the organisation I worked in, to avoid being displaced. I feared I wouldn't perform well at the interview, and it scared me. Realising I needed to make a change, whether I liked it or not, I had to take action. I got the job, but I ended up being miserable. I took the job for the sake of the job, then tried to get out of it, and ended up in a worse situation than the one I left. Because I didn't think about my own success criteria in that scenario, I couldn't have known beforehand whether the new role would be the right fit for me.

Establishing my success criteria in that situation could have entailed these steps:

- Determine what I wanted from the next job that I felt I was missing in my current one
- Define whether the type of work I wanted to spend most of my time on was developing new strategies or refining existing ones
- Clarify the type of organisation I wanted to work for. Do they exist solely to make a profit or are they driven by making a difference in the world?

Because I had not set those criteria, I ended up somewhere I didn't want to go, so it was a lot harder to recover and get back on the right path again than if I'd had them in place before I embarked on applying for the new role.

You may dispute the need for your own version of success criteria as you progress because you are a just-do-it person. If something goes wrong, you'll simply try again.

Typically, we keep raising the bar of expectations on ourselves and never feel happy, so setting success criteria is a deliberate happiness strategy. This is a way to value your time, make the most of it, and ensure it's not wasted by having to double back and retrace steps you've already taken in error.

EXERCISE 24

CONFIRMING YOUR SIMPLE SMART GOALS

Relax again in your preferred location and allow yourself thirty minutes. Make sure you have a copy of the SIMPLE SMART goals you set for yourself earlier (Chapter 5). If you haven't done so yet, return to Exercise 19 and complete it before you develop your success criteria below.

6: SUCCESS – WHAT DOES IT LOOK LIKE?

Your goals are essential items, along with your values, beliefs, and intentions, that will influence your success criteria. Complete the following worksheet with each of your goals, and the subgoals that are a part of that goal.

Success Criteria (Prioritisation) Worksheet

Below you will find a Success Criteria Prioritisation Worksheet where you can define what your success criteria are going to be. This will help you determine what and when you celebrate your successes. To demonstrate how to use it, there is an example based on the scenario provided in Exercise 19 of starting a community garden in rural Victoria.

In your case, if specific success criteria are not currently clear, complete each of the other columns first.

In Exercise 25, you will have the opportunity to focus specifically on the development of success criteria for your goals.

Example: Prioritisation Worksheet – Community Garden Project

GOAL	SUB-GOAL STEP	SUCCESS CRITERIA	PRIORITY/ ORDER TO ACTION
Find a suitable location to establish the community garden by end of 2025	Identify three potential locations to consider by July 2026	Three possible locations are identified.	1: Without this happening then other actions will not be needed.
	Identify real estate agents in potential locations by August 2026	Suitable real estate agents are identified.	2: Natural follow-on from finding a suitable location
	Visit potential locations and assess suitability by August 2026	Able to find three and assess their suitability to be able to narrow it down to two options.	4: Once criteria determined then it is possible to evaluate each site against the identified selection criteria
	Determine selection criteria to assess suitability of potential locations – mid-July to mid-August 2026		3: Once three options identified then assess against criteria

6: SUCCESS – WHAT DOES IT LOOK LIKE?

Please note that your items may not have as many sub-steps as this. It would be expected that each goal would have at least two sub-goal steps and no more than five. If there are more than five, you might want to consider whether you have two separate goals. These suggestions are only a guide, so be clear on what works best for you using, as necessary, the guidance that has been offered.

Blank Worksheet

You may want to make up your own worksheet as a Word document or a spreadsheet, depending on what you think works best for you.

GOAL	SUB-GOAL STEP	SUCCESS CRITERIA	PRIORITY/ ORDER TO ACTION

Here is another example of a SIMPLE SMART goal that serves as a guide to using the prioritisation worksheet. You might want to use this as a practice before undertaking the activity for your own SIMPLE SMART goals.

Let's say your SIMPLE SMART goal is to complete a master's degree in social justice, your main topic of interest, by the end of 2028. Achieving the sub-goals – the steps you must take to make that happen – becomes your initial set of success criteria.

Some of your success criteria could be:

- Identify universities that offer the course you are interested in.
- Review the topics to see if they suit your learning requirements (these are your learning-success criteria), which are: bring you up to date with the latest thinking; enable you to identify key issues in the topic area; allow you to apply your learnings in ways that align with your values and beliefs, such as extending diversity, positively influencing people's lives, most clearly align with your values and beliefs, etc.
- Investigate costs and payment options: Is it within the budget you have for learning and enhancing your knowledge?

6: SUCCESS - WHAT DOES IT LOOK LIKE?

- Contact the universities and speak to their academic advisors.
- Decide which course you prefer.
- Enrol in your preferred course.
- Start the coursework.
- Complete each subject within the course.
- Graduate.

Each of these steps can become success criteria. You might want to add others, or join two together as one.

Other success criteria may be less tangible, such as developing a community of practice in your area of interest through the course; broadening the cohort you can refer to regarding your area of interest; or gaining the ability to work in your chosen area, initially voluntarily. It is possible to measure each of these criteria, even if the measurement may not always be quantifiable.

If you find it difficult to work on your success criteria and sub-goals by yourself, you can always ask someone to assist you. As a master coach, I help clients to explore and develop their success criteria as they navigate their next paths.

MEASURING SUCCESS

Having defined your success criteria, or your checkpoints along the way, it's now time to consider valuable options for measuring success.

Establishing a measurement scale as a framework for determining if you're succeeding or not will help you to stay focused, and enable continued alignment to your goals. It is not about creating a burden for you to live with.

The framework can include tangible or quantifiable objective measures – you can touch them or put numbers against them. Let's say you're doing your master's course. One measure of success will be the number of subjects you've completed, for example, four out of twelve units after six months. Figures like this give you a clear indication of whether you're on track or not.

Intangible measures of success are qualitative and subjective, and rely on your own observations. In the case of studying, you could address this question: 'Is this course allowing me to be true to my values, and aligning with what I find meaningful?' You can give a yes-no response, or use a scale from 1–5, for example. You will decide which serves your framework best. It is difficult to know if you've succeeded if you have nothing to measure success against.

Let's return to Jill, whose story we first heard in Chapter 2. If she had not set success criteria, she would not have known whether she had achieved

6: SUCCESS – WHAT DOES IT LOOK LIKE?

her goal. She had at least two in place – 1) finish her MBA, and 2) get a more senior role in another organisation that was more aligned with her values. Those success criteria helped her to maintain focus and recognise when she had achieved her goal. She was able to celebrate her success and gain a sense of pride and momentum to do more.

At this point, you might be thinking, 'I don't know what success looks like for me,' so let's try a simple exercise. Think about something you want. Try not to overthink it. Small is good. It can be as simple as making a phone call you've been putting off. Satisfying that want is a success criterion for you.

EXERCISE 25
DETERMINING SUCCESS CRITERIA

Allow 20–30 minutes for this activity in your preferred location. Refer to the previous exercise where you thought about what success might look like for you, and consider your responses. Now, create success criteria for those responses. Remember, small is okay. If being altruistic is one of your ideas of success, then a simple success criterion could be to do one random act of kindness ten times over the next month.

If you have never thought about doing this before, and find it a little confronting, start with one success

> criterion. The goal, overall, may be five but starting with one is fine. Examples of success criteria are included in Exercise 24 (above). Review these to see if they help you to determine your own.
>
> Then give yourself a five-minute break and see if you can come up with another one. Don't push yourself too hard with this and don't rush it. Sometimes having time to stop and think about these things will allow the breakthrough to come.

DEVELOPING REFLECTIVE PRACTICES

You can enhance your intuition and fine-tune your ability to hear your own voice by sometimes reviewing your past actions and exploring what has worked and what you could improve upon, or simply providing time for your mind to rest.

Don't use these reflective practices to give yourself a hard time about what you did wrong, or to allow yourself to slack off mentally by becoming distracted and not focusing on the task at hand because it seems hard. Use your ideas and insights to your benefit, not your detriment. Enjoy the deliberate opportunities you create through these practices to tap into your intuition as you stop, pause, and take time to listen.

6: SUCCESS - WHAT DOES IT LOOK LIKE?

Categories of Reflective Practices

TYPE	FOCUS	EXPLANATION
Cognitive	Review your thoughts.	Discern what is helpful and what is not through deliberate thought processes.
Emotional	Understand that emotions provide data. What types of data do your emotions typically provide?	Learn to respond to situations rather than react.
Mindful	Take the time to notice what is going on around you.	Learn to listen with your eyes and not just your ears, and become aware of what is occurring around you.
Spiritual	Connect to the world with these mechanisms.	Engage through several avenues, which include nature, philosophical considerations, or religious practices, if appropriate.
Physical	Take time to hear what your body is telling you.	Understand what enables you to function well, and how you can know if and when you are under strain.

Through these activities, you will build a better awareness of yourself and your knowledge, skills, and competencies. Most importantly, they also enable you to tap into your intuition, a critical input helping you to determine what you want to do. Taking time out to tune into yourself is never a waste of time.

At the end of 2023, when I was still coming to terms with the loss of my husband, my second dad and a close friend suddenly passed away as well. I was required to face multiple life challenges, which led me to develop a persistent skin condition brought on by stress. Feeling alone and without help immediately on tap, like I had when my husband was alive, complicated the situation further. My turning point came when I realised I needed to find ways to manage my stress more effectively, and I began going down by the river to feel calmer and give my mind time to rest. This has become a form of spiritual reflection for me, as I take time out to connect with nature in the bigger world in which I live.

I also began writing a reflective journal using images and quotes to help me express my thoughts and make sense of what was occurring. The contemplative activity allowed me to think things through (a cognitive reflective practice) and to understand and learn how to regulate my emotions (an emotional reflective practice) more effectively.

Reflective practices provide you with quiet space to access your intuition and discern what is right for

6: SUCCESS – WHAT DOES IT LOOK LIKE?

you by closing down outside noise and turning up the focus on your own voice. Set aside time to do it instead of saying, 'I'm going to.' Actions speak louder than words and really enable progress along your next path.

You may be concerned that this activity will just cause you to feel bad about the mistakes you have made. Instead, choose to learn from experience and use this as a beneficial way to do it – a positive practice. You will also learn what matters to you now, in this stage of your life, and discern better alternatives for your future.

EXERCISE 26

REFLECTIVE PRACTICES WORKSHEET

Allow thirty minutes to complete your reflective practice using the worksheet included on the next page, in your favourite uninterrupted space. It's important not to rush the process. To develop a reflective-practice habit, start by doing this activity at least once a week. Over time, you might not need to do it so often as you get better at it; the frequency will be best determined by your need. Once you've become more practised at it, at least once a month will be beneficial.

Reflective Practices Worksheet

Step 1: Select an event that occurred over the last week or two that challenged you, and yet you succeeded in dealing with it, for example, having an important conversation with your manager about your contribution to the team.

Step 2: Answer the following questions. Refer to the explanations in italics in the first table to see how to use the worksheet.

QUESTION	RESPONSE
What was the challenging event?	Include a description of the challenging event – can be dot points and it does not have to be long.
What led you to approach the challenging event the way you did?	What factors influenced how you approached your challenging event? Assumptions? Mindsets? Fears and concerns?
Do you think you were successful? What did you do that may have led to you being successful or not?	What contributed to you being successful? • Personal input • Other party's input • Location • Timing • Other • Alignment to values • Alignment to intent and intentions

6: SUCCESS – WHAT DOES IT LOOK LIKE?

QUESTION	RESPONSE
Could what you did have been done differently/better? What steps will you put in place to ensure that you can achieve success in the future should this situation arise again?	What inhibited the degree of success you achieved? What ability did you have to influence (control) the level of success achieved? If you were doing this activity all over again, what would you do differently? What steps can you take? What help might you need to draw on? What about the environment would you need to change? Does the timing need to be reconsidered? Does who was involved need to change?

In your journal, complete the following questions about your specific challenging event.

QUESTION	RESPONSE
What was the challenging event?	
What led you to approach the challenging event the way you did?	

QUESTION	RESPONSE
Do you think you were successful? What did you do that may have led to you being successful or not?	
Could what you did have been done differently/better? What steps will you put in place to ensure that you can achieve success in the future should this situation arise again?	

If you are doubting the value of looking back at this point, consider this: Looking back enables you to identify what works for you and what doesn't, so you put more energy into what will benefit you the most going forward.

By giving yourself time to tune in to yourself along your journey, you can maintain focus and stay fuelled for the entire distance, not just part of it.

KEEPING YOUR INTENTIONS IN SIGHT

In Chapter 5, you spent time identifying your intentions. It is important to remember, though, that once revealed, they do not stay stagnant in that form. They further develop and evolve as you do, so it is

6: SUCCESS – WHAT DOES IT LOOK LIKE?

important to keep them in sight to maintain focus and direction. Write them down frequently, or place an image that reflects your intentions somewhere that will catch your eye every time you walk past it.

Remember, intentions do not have to be earth-shattering; they can be small, like becoming a more generous person. Your intentions positively contribute to your story. Unfortunately, with the extraneous noise we experience in life, we can lose sight of our best intentions, and that can be like driving with a blindfold on. If you don't ensure they are visible, you'll forget them. It's that simple.

For at least twenty years, I have had a desire to contribute to knowledge. That was my intention, but I was not attracting many opportunities to do that, partly because I hadn't kept it front of mind. I wasn't focusing my attention on ensuring it happened. I had previously contributed to knowledge by writing my thesis but when that was complete, I'd forgotten I had that intent.

Then I was unexpectedly invited by an independent educational institution to help develop a postgraduate course in coaching and leadership, which I happily said yes to.

About a year after the course was approved, the faculty leader then asked me to teach it. I needed to spend time listening to my voice and bringing back my intent, and when I did that the decision to take on teaching the course became a straightforward decision. I am now in my third year in that role, and broadening my reach by developing others as informed and reflective practitioner coaches.

As I decided whether to take on the teaching role offered to me, my intention was front of mind. Because I had documented 'contributing to knowledge' as something I wanted to do, and that had been a focus of my thinking, it informed my actions and ensured that my decision was aligned.

You might think that you will never forget your intentions, but the reality is, we all get busy and they slip from being foremost in our minds. I'm glad I had written mine down, so I could remind myself of them as needed. Based on what was happening in my life, I could then work out whether I needed to adjust or redefine them.

EXERCISE 27

SETTING INTENTIONS: SENTENCE-COMPLETION ACTIVITY

Allow fifteen minutes in your desired location and complete the following sentence in your journal: 'By the end of this year, I will have ...'

6: SUCCESS – WHAT DOES IT LOOK LIKE?

Add as many responses as you wish. For example, they could be:

- By the end of this year, I will have had at least four short three-day breaks.
- By the end of this year, I will have caught up every month with my closest friend.
- By the end of this year, I'll have received a promotion.
- By the end of this year, I'll have enjoyed three things on my bucket list.
- By the end of this year, I'll have finished reading three novels.

There are never too many responses to this statement, but you might want to prioritise. Once you've completed this exercise, it is important to place your statements in a location where you will see them often. Maybe print them out and stick them up on a wall, or use them as wallpaper on your phone. You could take a photo of them and look at it as often as you need to. Find a way that works for you, and make it easy for you to remind yourself often of what they are.

Continually add to your list. You might start with four or five items, and as time goes on, you might add another four or five. Be careful not to overwhelm yourself, but also don't limit yourself. You can add items that relate to different parts of your life, or add some based on the types of reflective practices you have. The options are endless, and the choice is yours.

> If you find it difficult to complete the sentence, think about just one thing you wish you could do this year. It might simply be visiting a friend, holidaying at a favourite location, or reading a book on a topic of interest. That can be your first answer to the question and your starting point, for example, 'By the end of the year, I will have visited my friend twice.' Then continue from there. If you can only come up with two or three, that is fine. Let the list grow over time if doing them all at once seems too difficult or overwhelming.

STAYING ON TRACK

Once you gain some momentum and begin implementing steps that will take you along your next path, things will likely come along to challenge you, some small, some big. It's good to have some effective strategies on hand to help you through.

There are two primary ways to stay on track: accountability mechanisms and feedback loops. Accountability means being committed to doing what you say you will do. Feedback loops ensure you continue to head in your desired direction.

Accountability does not imply punishment, and it is not onerous. Feedback loops ensure you remember to put your car lights on, so you are not driving in the dark and you have all the visibility you need to continue your journey.

6: SUCCESS – WHAT DOES IT LOOK LIKE?

Accountability provides the opportunity to be held to a certain standard or meet a certain expectation, and feedback loops are the mechanisms that review if you're on track or not. Developing an accountability framework and reviewing feedback loops ensures you stay on the course you chose, rather than straying onto a deviation you were not expecting.

The accountability factor that helped me reach an important education milestone was a little unusual. I had promised my husband, prior to his passing, that I would complete my PhD. Being a woman of my word and never making a promise I'm not willing to keep, I pressed on. He passed away before I finished and then I became consumed by grief. But never having broken a promise, especially not to my husband, I could not start now. He was my accountability measure.

Nine months after he passed away, I submitted my doctoral thesis. Six months later, they approved it. During the week that would have included his eightieth birthday, I became Dr Carol McGowan. This personal accountability measure provided a focus in a hard time, and gave me something to do that was constructive and had meaning for me, irrespective of the circumstances I found myself in. The same is true for any important accountability measure.

Feedback loops played a vital role for me when I was striving to reach another important goal – writing this book. The truth is, I find writing challenging – I do not know whether what I write is sufficient, and I am constantly picked up for poor grammar or being verbose. When I set the intent to write a book, knowing I had these challenges, I hired a book-writing mentor, and this provided me with regular reviews from someone more skilled than me to ensure I remained on track with subject matter and deadlines, and achieved my goal.

Without those regular feedback loops, I knew I would stagnate or procrastinate, either delaying completion of my book, or precluding me from finishing it at all. Suffice it to say, I'm glad I chose that route – and hopefully, you will be too when you set up the same support.

At this point, you might be thinking, 'I have accountability measures at work. Do I have to have them for myself?' Or, 'I cannot enforce accountability for myself, and I do not need feedback loops as I am a focused person.'

You can certainly set accountability measures for yourself. If your goals have meaning for you and staying on track is important to you, then keeping yourself accountable makes perfect sense. Even with the best of intentions, though, you can go off course. If you have feedback loops in place, you are less likely to do so.

EXERCISE 28

SETTING UP A PERSONAL ACCOUNTABILITY FRAMEWORK

Now you are going to establish how you plan to keep yourself accountable to the goals you have set for yourself.

For this task, allow yourself 60–90 minutes in your ideal location. I've developed the accountability-framework options structure below to assist with this process. You might even find sitting in a new location helpful for this exercise.

Accountability Framework Options

There is no one-size-fits-all approach to developing an accountability framework. Below is a list of options you can consider when setting out to establish your own. It can be formal or informal. This is not an exhaustive list.

FORMAL	PURPOSE	✓ IF APPROPRIATE FOR YOU
Set up an accountability partner	This is to provide you with the option of regularly checking in with someone you trust, a coach, or other form of helping professional You will need to agree on things such as: • Frequency • Location • Structure • Duration	
Reminder in calendar	You can set up a reminder in your calendar to do a regular check-in on your milestone points for your goals and objectives	
Use an app	There are apps that can be used to help you keep track of your goals and habits, e.g. Productive, a daily-habit tracker	
Include a copy of your timeline where it is highly visible for you to see	Keeps your goals and objectives present front of mind	

6: SUCCESS – WHAT DOES IT LOOK LIKE?

INFORMAL	PURPOSE	✓ IF APPROPRIATE FOR YOU
Daily affirmations	These help to remind you of your intent and intentions by regularly affirming what you intend to do	
Time for reflection	This is to allow you to take time to stop and reflect on what you have done and especially what you are proud of	
Future image	Find an image or make a drawing that reflects your desired future state and put it where you can easily see it; this will help to keep your goals and objectives present front of mind	
Other – formal or informal	Any other options you can devise that will help to keep you accountable and on the path towards your next goal	

Select the approaches you want to use by placing ✓ beside those you deem most appropriate for meeting your needs and your personality type. Include a date when you plan to use this accountability approach for the first time.

For the first 30-45 minutes, review the accountability framework options. Look at the options provided, then develop your own items that align with your goals, values, and beliefs.

Once you've completed your worksheet, take the next fifteen minutes to do the following:

- Set in place your accountability measures and an initial date and time for feedback, either by yourself, with others, or using your electronic mechanisms.
- Schedule these dates in your calendar and act on them as your highest priority.
- Document results of your first feedback and outcomes in your journal.

As the final part of this activity, answer the following questions:

- What have you learned or discovered?
- What did you need to revise?

You might be wondering, 'I don't know if I want to do this. I'm not sure it's worth the effort.' Determine one obvious risk if you do not stay the course, like reverting to a life that contains no excitement. Will this matter to you? If yes, then establishing accountability measures and feedback loops will reduce the likelihood of that risk happening.

6: SUCCESS – WHAT DOES IT LOOK LIKE?

CONCLUSION

This chapter has identified ways you will know when you've succeeded and stayed on course. We looked at:

- Meaningful measures of success
- Enhancing, discovering, and developing reflective practices that help you enhance your intuition and ability to hear your own voice
- How to keep your intentions front of mind
- Staying on track by using personal and objective accountability measures and feedback loops

Establish mechanisms that will help you stay the course, and the checkpoints you need to ensure you stay on track.

Now that you can determine what success looks like, the next chapter will reveal how to celebrate that success and stay inspired throughout the journey, even if there are detours. Let's party!

CELEBRATE SUCCESS

Remember to take time out to celebrate small and large successes as you focus and dedicate time to navigating your next path. Pause now and then to reflect on where you are, then acknowledge yourself (most importantly) and others for what you have achieved.

Let's look at why it is important to acknowledge and celebrate the many small steps you achieve along the way, for example, self-advocating when feeling you were being ignored or disadvantaged in a sticky situation. You must create different celebrations to keep you inspired by the progress you have made, instead of berating yourself for what you have not done.

When things are tough, I take five to ten minutes to acknowledge one small step I've taken that day that has moved me a step closer to where I want to be. It might simply be making a phone call, but even that can be big if I'm feeling it's all a bit too hard.

Celebrating success helps you to increase your confidence levels and keeps you focused on what you were aiming for – one of the key things I learned through my studies in positive psychology.

Celebrating success helps you build your resiliency muscles. As Oprah Winfrey once said, 'The more you praise and celebrate your life, the more there is in life to celebrate.'

Kathryn Bryant and Julian Illman, authors of the book *Changeability*, focus on helping people develop the ingredients for happy and fulfilled lives. Bryant and Illman, on their Brilliant Living HQ website, outline that celebrations of successes lead to at least five positive results:

1. They provide the opportunity for you to learn and adapt so you can replicate the good results in the future.
2. They enable you to develop and grow your success mindset.
3. Celebrations help you to maintain inspiration and motivation.
4. They help you feel good, releasing healthy hormones such as dopamine into your system.
5. Celebrating success not only benefits you, it provides benefits for others even if you are just telling them about how you are celebrating your success.

7: CELEBRATE SUCCESS

Celebrations are not luxuries; they're healthy medicines we can administer to ourselves with no need for a prescription.

In the previous chapter, you outlined what success looks like for you, so now let's look at ways to celebrate those successes, why celebrating is a necessity, how celebrating with others has compounding positive effects, and how frequently you will need to celebrate to keep you sustained as you travel along your next path.

WHY CELEBRATE SUCCESS?

Celebrating success is not a nice-to-have; it's a necessity that will help you stay committed to the task and enhance your positive wellbeing. Significance is not the sole criterion to determine if something deserves to be celebrated. Learning a new skill, helping someone reach a deadline without being asked, or doing something you did not think you could do are all achievements that deserve acknowledgement this way.

Celebrating is a form of honouring yourself and showing respect for what you've done. This is not about having a party for the sake of it, or finding an excuse for a night out on the town. How you choose to celebrate will vary, from a low-key conversation to an extravagant party, and a wide range of other options in between. If you're an introvert, you might prefer something quiet, whereas an extrovert might prefer something with greater fanfare.

Any type of celebration provides time for you to take stock and reflect on lessons learned along the way, and also strengthens your connections to people, resources, and other useful tools that will make your further achievements not only probable but definite possibilities.

Do you want to feel confident that you *will* achieve deep-seated fulfilment? Celebrating success on the way will help ensure you do. It's like drinking a healthy tonic, giving you the stamina to stay the course. Taken in regular doses that align with the significance you place on what you've achieved, you will keep going for as long as you want and need to.

Also, celebrating minor achievements provides fuel for reaching bigger goals and targets. Not taking time out to celebrate is like not keeping a vital machine well oiled; it won't keep working as it's meant to. In humans, this can manifest as tiredness, and possibly mental exhaustion, as our bodies release harmful hormones. If you avoid taking time out to acknowledge achievements for too long, you can risk burnout.

Celebrating success helps you keep going when the going is tough, as well as when it's favourable. The feeling of achievement helps release more good hormones, such as dopamine, providing the tonic you need – apart from the obvious fun you will have when you celebrate.

7: CELEBRATE SUCCESS

Francisco Sáez, in his article 'Micro-Tasks. The Pleasure of Checking Off', says:

> 'The reason is that whenever you recognise a task or project as completed, your brain releases a load of dopamine, a neurotransmitter that is responsible for generating feelings of accomplishment, satisfaction and happiness. The release of dopamine not only makes you feel good but also motivates you to continue completing tasks and extend that pleasure of feeling.'

At this point, you might wonder, 'Do I celebrate everything I achieve? That could be time-consuming.' In Chapter 7, you developed your success criteria, so use them as milestones for achievements you want to celebrate. Pick one that is important to you and start with that. (If an activity was simply routine, like making a regular phone call, recognise it with 'Well done'; it probably does not warrant much more time than that.)

EXERCISE 29

ACHIEVEMENTS LOG

Take thirty minutes in your preferred location when you know you're unlikely to be interrupted. In your journal, note five things you've achieved in the last month. If you feel that is too many, start with one.

Spend several minutes savouring what you've been able to achieve because this will regulate your emotions to generate, enhance or maintain any positive emotions you experience. (This is achieved by mindful acknowledgement and recognition of different life experiences.)

You might want to write down big achievements in larger writing and smaller ones in smaller writing, so that when you look at them, they're relatively obvious. Take time to notice how you feel now, compared to before starting this activity.

In your journal, record what feels different for you because of documenting five of your achievements. Write down any realisations you've had because of this exercise. You will apply these insights to later exercises in this chapter.

Maybe you're thinking, 'I have achieved little over the last month. My work and life are just routine. There is not much variation.' In that case, think of one thing you did in the last month that differed from your general routine. What was it and what did you achieve because of that one variation?

THE BENEFITS OF CELEBRATING WITH OTHERS

There are some things we do need to do on our own – but connecting with others is crucial for our health and wellbeing. Celebrating success alone is good, but doing it with others is even better as it provides enhanced positive input, such as encouragement and inspiration to keep going. It helps you stay connected and stay the course.

This does not mean you have a big party every time you achieve something – that would be overkill for some but not for others. Choose what's right for you to enhance and foster positive connections. It is not only you who benefits; they do, too, through a beneficial wave effect. It is unlikely you've achieved your successes on your own, so celebrating with others can be one way of acknowledging their contribution.

Celebrating success with others can enhance a variety of important factors in your life. After researching the impact of celebrating success, I've created a table that outlines the benefits, explaining them and determining whether they are best undertaken by celebrating individually or with others.

LIFE'S NEXT PATH

Benefits of Success

BENEFITS OF CELEBRATING SUCCESS	EXPLANATION	INDIVIDUAL	WITH OTHERS
Appreciation	Recognising and enjoying the good qualities of someone or something	✓	✓
Unity	Being joined to something		✓
Connectedness	Having a sense of belonging or affinity with others		✓
Understanding	Developing self-awareness and knowledge of what matters to you	✓	✓
Purpose and commitment	Finding what gives you meaning and the impetus to keep going and press on	✓	✓

Accountability	A willingness to accept responsibility and to account for your actions as required	✓	✓
Growing gratitude	Being thankful for what you have; showing appreciation for the good in your life	✓	
Enhancing self-worth and self-efficacy	Your belief in your ability to succeed, and belief that you deserve the good in your life	✓	

As I wrote this book, I needed a definite deadline, and I needed a way to ensure that I finished the manuscript. Consequently, when I finished writing I celebrated with all those who made it possible, starting with my book mentor and all others who supported me, either practically or emotionally. That included those who continually reminded me I could do this – and I needed that often, believe me. Without all of them, this would not have happened. I celebrated with them in feasible ways, given proximity and level of contribution. Writing a book is not a solo journey, and I needed to celebrate with those who helped me get there. As the saying goes, 'It takes a village to raise a child.' (And create a book.)

Your achievements so far have most likely resulted from your efforts and others' input, so take time to recognise what you have done, and acknowledge those who may have helped make it happen. It will benefit all of you.

You might be thinking at this point, 'I've done everything on my own, no one helped me.' Believe me, someone somewhere has helped you – someone milked the cow so you could have it in your coffee this morning. Or pressed a soybean. Or harvested oats. Maybe you could think a bit more broadly and see who you come up with.

EXERCISE 30

ACHIEVEMENT CELEBRATION GUIDE – PART 1

Take thirty uninterrupted minutes in your favourite location. Review the achievements you listed in the previous exercise, and create a table with two columns, one titled Achievement and the other titled 'Who Was Involved Other Than Me?'. Fill that out, and you have identified the achievements

7: CELEBRATE SUCCESS

you wish to celebrate, and who you will celebrate with. You will then use this information in the next exercise to develop your celebration calendar.

Example of how to complete this sheet:

ACHIEVEMENT	WHO WAS INVOLVED OTHER THAN ME?
Completed first edit of book	Writing buddy and book coach
Gave titles to all the exercises in the book	Book coach
Developed book cover	Book coach, graphic designers, marketer, friends, and potential readers

Now it's time for you to complete the first part of your Achievement Celebration Guide:

ACHIEVEMENT	WHO WAS INVOLVED OTHER THAN ME?

> Instead of worrying whether this is taking time away from achieving your goals, think of it as putting on your oxygen mask so you can breathe more easily when you reach the next levels of your journey.

CELEBRATION FREQUENCY AND TYPE

How often will you need to celebrate success, and what types of celebrations do you want to enjoy so you feel sustained and keen to keep going on your new path?

Throughout writing this book, I decided I wanted to celebrate my successes by enjoying an entertainment activity at least once a fortnight. This could have been a movie or musical, depending on what was on, its location, and timing. Sometimes I went with friends and other times I went alone. There was no specific rhyme or reason for that choice: sometimes it felt good to do it alone, and other times I went alone because other people were busy. Irrespective of that, each event was pleasant and provided me with a treat that I enjoyed.

The acts of celebrating success, and determining the frequency of them, are not meant to burden you but give you something to look forward to. It is not about reaching a destination; it's about enjoying the journey you are on and where it is taking you. I felt if I went to a show more than once a fortnight, it would have been a strain both physically and financially, and that would have defeated the purpose of doing it.

7: CELEBRATE SUCCESS

Rewards do not have to be frequent or expensive, but they do need to have some significance for you:

- Celebrate the small steps in small or large ways, depending on what you consider relevant.
- Celebrate regularly and as often as suits you. For me, it was at least fortnightly.
- Reward yourself, but also reward others who may have helped you. This could simply be a thank-you for some, or a meal out, or some other mutually enjoyable activity for others.
- Determine what you feel is relevant to celebrate alone, and what deserves celebration with others. (That is not always based on the size of the achievement.) I found the entertainment event allowed me to do it on my own, and with others as circumstances permitted and warranted.

Other ways to celebrate success could be:

- Spending time with people you care about over coffee or a meal
- Showing appreciation and saying thank you
- Expressing your creativity by doing something artistic or colourful
- Practising and expressing appreciation for what you have

- Allowing yourself to be spontaneous and letting the mood take you where it will, for example, jumping in your car and driving to a location you enjoy. (I always take myself somewhere where there is water.)

Remember to include activities that you and, as appropriate, others also find enjoyable.

Celebration helps to keep fuel in your tank. Figure out the things you want to celebrate both for yourself and with those you wish to include. If celebrating is not something you have done a lot of, it might be time to learn to celebrate a little more.

Formal celebrations, like graduations or award ceremonies, are predefined by others. You can easily plan informal celebrations like a picnic or an outing with a friend for a favourite occasion. All celebrations help us move forward.

The *Psychology Today* online article titled 'From Small Steps to Big Wins' on 12 June 2024 states:

> '… celebrating wins activates the brain's reward system, boosting motivation, e.g. life satisfaction.' They go on to say: 'Recognising small helps solidify lessons learned, fostering intentional future actions.'

Yes, it is important to celebrate wins no matter how big or small.

7: CELEBRATE SUCCESS

You might be resisting the idea of celebrating, thinking you hate fuss. If you achieve something that takes you in the direction you want to go, then it's worth celebrating in some way that is meaningful to you.

EXERCISE 31

ACHIEVEMENT CELEBRATION GUIDE – PART 2

Taking thirty uninterrupted minutes in your favourite location, add two more columns titled Options to Celebrate and Possible Timeframe to the table you created in the previous exercise. Be mindful not to overload yourself, as the last thing you want to do is make it a burden. Develop a celebration calendar that you will enjoy.

Using the same example from Exercise 30, here is the extended version of the Celebrating Success Table.

ACHIEVEMENT	OTHERS INVOLVED	OPTIONS TO CELEBRATE	POSSIBLE TIMEFRAME
Completed first edit of book	Writing buddy and book coach	Have a meal together Go to a show together	1–2 months from completion
Gave titles to all the exercises in the book	Book coach	Celebratory drink Watch a favourite TV show	From 1–3 days
Developed book cover	Book coach, graphic designers, marketer, friends and potential readers	Share it with friends and enjoy their responses Have a Zoom meeting with book coach and have a coffee together to celebrate our mutual achievement	Over 2–4 weeks

7: CELEBRATE SUCCESS

Celebrating Success Table

Now it's time for you to complete the second part of your Achievement Celebration Guide.

ACHIEVEMENT	OTHERS INVOLVED	OPTIONS TO CELEBRATE	POSSIBLE TIMEFRAME

Maybe you don't see the value in scheduling celebrations – can't they just happen when the mood strikes? They can, but that might not provide you with all the fuel you need to keep you forging forward.

CONCLUSION

In this chapter, we looked at:

- Why we need to celebrate success
- The value of celebrating success with others
- Determining the frequency and type of celebrations that will provide fuel for your journey

LIFE'S NEXT PATH

Celebrate and acknowledge your progress so you stay focused on navigating your next path, leading you to your desired destination.

BRINGING IT ALL TOGETHER

As stated in the introduction to this book, all of the ideas, exercises, and suggestions in this book are informed by the application of the integrated Strategic Achievement Framework that is made up of strategic intent, strategic action, and strategic intuition.

While each part of the framework has value on its own, they are even more powerful when combined. Each step you take will help inform the next – each iteration is like an upward spiral taking you closer to your desired destination.

STRATEGIC INTENT

The first component of the framework, strategic intent, clarifies and defines what you want to achieve and why. Your intent is strategic because it's rooted in what truly matters to you, as revealed through the exercises in Chapters 1–6. You've invested thoughtful consideration into identifying your goals.

Strategic intent is about clearly articulating your desires, ensuring you are decisive about what you want. It guides you in determining where to focus your energy, helping you stay on track as you work toward successfully navigating your next path.

A clear understanding of what you want to achieve and why will keep you focused on the path, increasing your chances of reaching your desired destination. Your intent is the bullseye you're aiming for.

EXERCISE 32

AMALGAMATE CHAPTERS 1–4 (YOUR INTENT)

Allow thirty minutes to one hour for this activity. Gather your responses from the exercises you completed in Chapters 1–4. If it helps, photocopy pages from your journal or do a printout if you have typed up your responses. Place each exercise on a table, then sort them into an order or categories that make sense to you.

Take your time with this exercise, allowing your head and heart to guide you. Observe the order in which your thoughts and feelings arise and use this to shape your intent.

During this reflection, document what you've discovered about what truly matters to you. This will be your first attempt at articulating your desired intent.

If you find yourself struggling, thinking, 'I don't have anything from my exercises that will help with this,' start by selecting just two items from those earlier activities. Look for any common threads in what you've identified. Once you have a starting point, continue adding to it and see what emerges.

STRATEGIC ACTION

The second component of the framework is strategic action – the steps you'll take to achieve your strategic intent. These actions are carefully designed to support your growth as you progress toward your next big goal, building on the concepts discussed in Chapters 5–7. These aren't just random steps; they form a coordinated and integrated plan rooted in your strategic intent to guide you toward your goals.

EXERCISE 33

AMALGAMATE CHAPTERS 5–7 (YOUR ACTION)

Without a plan, turning your strategic intent into strategic action is challenging. To begin, find a quiet, uninterrupted space to spend thirty minutes to an hour. Bring all your responses from Chapters 5–7, along with the results of each activity.

You might wonder, 'Do I really need to do this? Can't I just keep it in my head?' The answer depends on how committed you are to success. Skipping this step might compromise your ability to reach your next important goal.

Strategic intent and strategic action are the more straightforward parts of this process. However, in the next section, we'll explore strategic intuition, a less commonly considered aspect of planning. This is the secret ingredient – the 'secret sauce' – that often goes unmentioned but is crucial for focusing on what you truly want and desire

7: BRINGING IT ALL TOGETHER

STRATEGIC INTUITION

Strategic intuition is the third component of the framework. We have looked at this topic in Chapters 1, 4, and 6, where you explored meaning and purpose in your life. Now, let's deepen your understanding and help you apply this to the work you have already done.

Strategic intuition makes the difference. Rational thinking and emotions are useful data, but your intuition, which has never let you down, will make the key difference in you being able to successfully navigate your next path.

EXERCISE 34

YOUR INTUITION

Set aside thirty minutes in your chosen location, where you can focus with no interruptions. If you can, find a place with a pleasant view while you ponder your responses.

Return to your answers from the exercise at the start of this chapter where you reviewed the activities from Chapters 1, 4, and 6, in which you tackled ideas like meaning and purpose, and double-checked them to make sure they were truly intuitive and not reactive (instinctive) or a gut feeling.

Now that you have a more detailed understanding of the overall framework, have your responses changed because of this new understanding? If so, make the necessary adaptations to your responses.

Once you've done this, you might like to take one step further. Use one sentence to summarise your strategic-intent element, one sentence for your strategic-action element, and one sentence for your strategic-intuition element. How would you combine all three sentences to make one statement about your strategic-achievement plan? This could be the mantra you use to keep you focused on your next exciting journey.

Using my decision to undertake a pastoral counselling course as an example, my sentences would be as follows:

- Strategic intent: Learn more about what counselling entails.
- Strategic action: Attend the pastoral counselling course as an introduction.
- Strategic intuition: My intuition indicated that this would provide insights about counselling that I did not fully understand at this point without being overwhelming. It was a good way to dip my toe in the water.

7: BRINGING IT ALL TOGETHER

One Sentence:

My intuition told me that attending the pastoral counselling course would help me see if I wanted to pursue more formal studies in this field, and by doing so, I hoped to spend my time wisely and move in the right direction.

Your sentences:

CONCLUSION: SET FORTH

It's never too late to make a shift and have a renewed purpose in your life. Imagine waking up and experiencing fulfilment that is profound and lucent. What does that look like?

You get up and have breakfast like the rest of the world, but inside you're feeling energy and enthusiasm for what's ahead in your day. Does that mean you love every single meeting and every single person you meet or work with? Maybe not – or maybe it does.

You are feeling so clear about your purpose and your journey along your next path that you feel a sense of graciousness and enthusiasm toward everyone and everything. Everyone you meet and everything you do is taking you towards a goal that excites and motivates you.

You know exactly where you are heading and why you are heading there because of the knowledge and determination you've built up by reading this book and completing the exercises along the way.

You feel a sense of energy and purpose. To achieve the change you desire, you must respond to the call.

Learn where to start (strategic intent), hear your own story and listen to your inner voice (strategic intent and intuition), get equipped for the journey (strategic action), plan the best route (strategic action and intuition), and celebrate all the steps along the way (strategic action).

There may be obstacles and barriers. You may fall back into old habits and lose momentum along the way. If this happens, you're not alone. The journey along your next path will have setbacks.

If that happens, check in on your progress by reviewing the exercises you've completed so far, and to regain momentum, remind yourself of the success you've had so far.

Good luck, and may you travel your NEXT path in tip-top condition, where radiant and radical fulfilment awaits you.

Author note: You can download free life navigation resources and the first three exercises in this book (a fillable pdf) here: www.strategicachievementcoaching.com.au/resources

INVITATION FROM CAROL

Please join me as I build a community of accomplished people who simply refuse to stay stuck and who are successfully travelling their next path. They're not letting their current or previous successes be a double-edged sword. They're taking more risks.

You have everything you need in this book. However, if you want my help, contact me. This is what I do – help people imagine and achieve their next big thing. Journeys are more fun when you have someone to travel with, celebrate with, and to help navigate challenges you might encounter along the way.

Carol McGowan – Strategic Achievement Coaching

Website: www.strategicachievementcoaching.com.au

LinkedIn: www.linkedin.com/in/carol-mcgowan-phd

Email: carol@strategicachievementcoaching.com.au

LIFE'S NEXT PATH

Not everyone has the courage and conviction to embark on the journey along their next path. Will you be one of them? For those who dare to step out, I wish you great fulfilment as you navigate the path.

Imagine a world where everyone achieves this profound sense of purpose and joy – where each of us reaches our next big goal.

The choice is yours: Do you want to live with fulfilment, or drift through life in a daze? The power to decide is in your hands.

ACKNOWLEDGEMENTS

I want to acknowledge four specific groups of people, as well as individuals I value.

Book Guides – to Kath Walters for helping me develop a workable manuscript in 90 days; and Bev Ryan for helping to finesse the words and create a book worth presenting to others. Thank you both for helping me become an author. Your input, support, and encouragement have been invaluable. I could not have done it without you.

Business Guides – to Linda Johannesson for helping me define and develop my work as a coach and an author; and Cecilia Moar for helping me get the message out about what I do and why I do it. You have both helped me learn the importance of consistently themed messages over time.

Professional Guides – to the two people I turn to for help to continue to grow and inform how I show up: Sue Langley, for being so passionate about Positive Psychology and helping others understand its benefits; and Dr David Drake for learning how to mature no matter how old you are, and appreciating the value of your own story. Thank you both for your insights. They are life-changing, and I am one very grateful recipient of your wisdom.

Life Support Crew – let me start with three women I call my 'tripod', as they hold me up through the vagaries of life, and deserve a special mention:
- Dr Pauline Ross, who cares so much that she ensures I am doing okay every day, with chats and wisdom that has leached into the topics discussed in this book
- Gail McGarry, my buddy. I call us an unexpected 'salt and pepper' pairing – she is the salt; I am the pepper. Her presence and love add flavour and spice every day, and I cannot imagine my life without her.
- Colleen Lewis, my international counterpart and dear friend. We have only met online and yet the relationship is very deep and real. We speak every week and support each other through the ups and downs of life that manage to crop up more consistently than either of us would like.

'Thank you' seems inadequate when stating what you mean to me. I would not have reached this point without your unwavering belief in my ability to write this book.

7: ACKNOWLEDGEMENTS

There are several other important people I would like to acknowledge as part of my life support crew:

- Paul van Hauen, Matt Kay and Jim McGarry, the men who provided strength and support of a different kind.
- Dr Lynn Scoles, who started the writing journey with me and each week shared her time while we each worked on our own books
- Dr Andrew Beshara and Deborah Rollings, who provided medical support and counselling while I was writing this book, as I navigated a very difficult phase in my life that went on much longer than I would have liked

To those I have not mentioned specifically, please know I value you and what you contribute to my life as friends, family, colleagues or business acquaintances.

Finally, thank you to all those who chose to read this book. I hope you find it to be a valuable resource as you navigate your next steps.

www.ingramcontent.com/pod-product-compliance
Lightning Source LLC
Chambersburg PA
CBHW061745070526
44585CB00025B/2812